Brides

COMPANION

"For my fiancé, with love"

MQ Publications Limited
12 The Ivories, 6–8 Northampton Street
London N1 2HY
Tel: +44 (0) 20 7359 2244
Fax: +44 (0) 20 7359 1616
email: mail@mqpublications.com
www.mqpublications.com

Copyright © 2005 MQ Publications Limited
Text copyright © 2005 Susannah Marriott

ISBN: 1-84072-779-9

1 3 5 7 9 0 8 6 4 2

Printed and bound in China

Brides

COMPANION

SUSANNAH MARRIOTT

MQP

Contents

6 Introduction • 10 Setting the Date • 12 A Girl's Best Friend • 14 Unusual Places to Get Married • 18 Precious Proposals • 20 Bridal Birthstones • 22 "Although I conquer all the earth" • 24 Making a Beaded Comb • 28 Unfortunate Coincidence • 30 *Beauty and the Beast* • 36 The Language of Flowers • 38 Pin Money • 39 Pillar of Salt • 40 Pearls of Love • 42 Something Old, Something New • 46 "Married when the year is new" • 48 Good-Luck Charms • 54 Light of My Life • 56 Jumping the Broom • 58 The Trousseau • 62 *The Tales of Chekhov* • 64 The Hope Chest • 68 The Meaning of Flowers • 70 *Love's Philosophy* • 72 Crystallizing Rose Petals • 74 Herbal Lore for Bouquets • 76 *My True Love Hath My Heart* • 78 Spring Floral Displays • 80 Spring Flowers for Bouquets • 82 Divination to Find a Husband • 84 Love Divination Rhyme for Daisy Petals • 86 Fairytale Weddings • 90 The Rationed Bride • 94 Welsh Love Spoons • 96 The Lover's Knot • 98 Defiant Elopement • 102 Shedding a Tear • 104 Bride Quilts • 106 Traditional Bride Quilt Motifs • 108 *The Quilters* • 110 The Bachelorette Party • 113 Bridal Showers • 114 Shower Themes • 116 Champagne Cocktail • 117 Pitchers of Iced Tea • 120 The Wedding Brunch • 122 Outdoor Decor • 126 A Canopy • 128 Outdoor Celebrations • 130 *My Mother's House* • 134 Dressing a Party Tent • 138 Wedding Favors • 140 Classic Cocktails • 142 Domestic Goddesses • 144 If Music Be the Food of love… • 146 *He Will Praise His Lady* • 148 Dressing Tiny Bridesmaids • 150 Making a Bridesmaid's Flower Ball • 152 Summer Floral Displays • 154 Apache Marriage Song • 156 Summer Flowers for Bouquets • 158 Lady in Red • 160 *Dorani* • 166 The Dress • 170 Taking the Veil

• **174** Making a Boutonnière • **176** Flowers for Boutonnières • **178** All White • **180** "Marry in white you've chosen right" • **182** The Bridal Crown • **184** Orange Blossom • **186** Vintage Style That Works • **188** Wash that Man Right Out of Your Hair! • **190** Prewedding Skin Scrub • **192** Lulur Body Scrub • **193** A Wedding Morning Ritual • **194** "I wear your golden ring, my dear" • **196** Faith Rings • **198** The Wedding Ring • **200** "With these rings I thee wed" • **202** Band of Gold • **204** Making a Table Centerpiece • **208** Scented Party Favors • **209** Old-Fashioned Lemonade • **212** Continental Wedding Cakes • **216** Out with the Old • **218** *Anna Karenina* • **222** Choosing Champagne • **224** Traditional Wedding Toasts • **226** Aphrodisiacs for Wedding Feasts • **230** Jackie Kennedy's Wedding • **232** Fall Floral Displays • **234** Fall Flowers for Bouquets • **236** Love Divination Rhyme for Cherry Stones • **238** Fruitful Unions • **240** *Emma* • **244** Tiered Cakes • **246** The Wedding Cake • **248** Making a Napkin Ring • **250** Leaving the Ceremony • **252** Russian Wedding Procession • **254** That Kiss • **256** Casting Confetti • **258** "Green" Confetti • **260** Make Some Noise • **262** *Les Misérables* • **266** Love Letters • **268** Tossing the Bouquet • **272** The Language of Roses • **274** *The Return of the Native* • **276** "Saturday night shall be my whole care" • **278** Meditation for the Night Before • **280** The Wedding Night Bed • **282** Scenting the Bridal Bed • **284** Choosing Linen • **286** Decorating the Table • **287** Winter Floral Display • **288** Winter Flowers for Bouquets • **292** *A Chaparral Christmas Gift* • **294** The Captive Bride • **296** Who Not to Marry • **298** Making Thank You Cards • **300** Threshold Traditions • **302** The Honeymoon

Introduction

I collect weddings. Come Saturday afternoon you'll find me lurking in churchyards or hanging out at the local Russian Baths to spy on Bengali wedding planners struggling to secure groaning canopies of flowers to ornate plastic columns. Sundays I'm out waving at Turkish brides in their flower-and-ribbon drenched stretch limos as they speed, horn honking, down main street.

I've been invited to more than a few amazing weddings over the years: the Greek wedding where the bride's veil caught fire as man and wife took their first steps together around the altar; the mendhi ceremony where we women, dressed in traditional Indian clothes, banged drums, danced suggestively, and sang ribald songs around the frankly disgusted bride-to-be, who could do nothing but sit motionless in her shabbiest clothes as her hands and feet were painted with henna; and the curry-in-a-bucket reception with reggae sound system (we broke down in the camper van there and back); there was a tango wedding (with a honeymoon in Buenos Aires) when the bride and groom performed the most intimate dance and us girls dissolved into tears (no one would ever love us that much), then gorged on chocolate cake from the city's finest French patisserie; the daffodil wedding in a piano museum with harpsichord accompaniment where the best man was a woman (me); and there I was, dressed to the nines again, witnessing a two-hour Ghanian ceremony, the bargaining over the bride price by two sets of elders dressed in *kente* cloth getting ever more theatrical (she's got a degree; he has a British passport).

I savor the less showy occasions, too: on a whim in Lake Tahoe with kids, dressed from the nearest thrift shop (I watched that one on video); the simple town hall wedding where the blooming bride (eight months pregnant) and groom looked so dazzlingly, astonishingly happy that all assembled rose to cheer at "I will"; the quiet wedding breakfast in a room above a bar, serving just sushi (from her homeland) and pork pies (from his). What made all these weddings special was the way the ceremony and subsequent celebrations reflected the personality, heritage, and sheer bloodymindedness of the couple, who were able to resist the onslaught of expectation from parents, wedding planners, marquee-hire staff, poached-salmon caterers, and dodgy DJs. I hope this compendium of wedding lore, and ideas for flowers and food, decor and dresses, readings and rings will provide inspiration for you to make your wedding day your very own.

"I sing of maypoles, hock-carts, wassails, wakes, Of bridesgrooms, brides and of the bridal cakes."

from *Hesperides* by Robert Herrick

Setting the Date

It is considered the bride's prerogative to choose the day of her wedding. But selecting a traditionally lucky date could not be more tricky. In parts of Scotland, it is still said that you should marry while the moon is waxing, not waning, as was common advice throughout medieval England—"A growing moon and a flowing tide are lucky times to marry in" goes the proverb. In India, it is left to astrologers to decree an auspicious time for nuptials by the stars, and here, too, it is said that a marriage begins with plenty of good fortune if there is a full moon a day before the wedding. In medieval England, so-called "dismal days," those considered unlucky for weddings, were set by the church, and the tradition lingers today. Precluded dates included Fridays (the day of Christ's Crucifixion), the periods from Advent Sunday to eight days after Epiphany, Septuagesima Sunday to the eighth day after Easter, the Sunday before Ascension Day to the eighth day after Pentecost. Unauthorized marriages during these times could lead to prosecution. And then

there was the farmer's adage that "They that wive between sickle and scythe shall never thrive," setting harvest time out of limits. When Puritans strictly enforced Sunday as a day of rest, this weekday was verboten too. In Italy, by contrast, Sunday is felt to be the luckiest day of the week for a wedding.

A Girl's Best Friend

"He, who having a pure body, always carries a diamond with sharp points, without blemish, free from all faults; that one, as long as he lives, knows each day will bear some things: happiness, prosperity, children, riches, grain, cows, and meat. He who wears [such] a diamond will see dangers recede from him whether he be threatened by serpents, fire, poison, sickness, thieves, flood or evil spirits."

from the *Ratnapariksa* of Buddha Bhatta, sixth century

The king of jewels, the diamond, is said in Italy to be forged from the flames of love. Indian gemlore states that the stone concentrates within it the energy of the sun and has the ability to boost sexual performance. The stone's very name, from the Greek *adamao*, means "I conquer" because of its immense strength and hardness, making it a worthy symbol for the worth and durability of a love match. Its peerless quality is another attribute that suits it to tributes of devotion. So rare and esteemed are diamonds that in thirteenth-century France, Louis IX reserved their use for the king alone, a decree echoed in sixth-century India. Diamonds are thought to have aphrodisiac properties that attract beauty, power, and charm to the wearer (certainly the men who proffer them seem to have an irresistible allure). Wearing the stone is also thought to be strengthening for the reproductive system. Diamonds are reputed to enhance creativity and almost everywhere around the globe to offer protection from evil.

Unusual Places to Get Married

Browse specialist books and Web sites to find details of extra-special venues licensed for marriage ceremonies. Here's some inspiration for those who hanker to be a bikini bride on the beach or haul adventurous guests halfway up a mountain.

Classically romantic venues
Follies and fairytale castles; rural parish churches and cathedrals; Benedictine abbeys and holy islands; stately homes, manor houses, and orangeries; sunset beaches and private islands

Historic buildings
Napoleonic forts and coachhouses; barns and farmhouses; galleries and museums; railway stations and golf courses; old film studios or cinemas and casinos

Outdoor venues
Formal landscaped gardens; orchards and wildflower meadows; football stadia and zoos; hot tubs and saunas

Spectacular natural settings
On the shore of a lake or overlooking a waterfall; in underground caverns, coal or tin mines; within stone circles and on ancient hill forts; while scubadiving or skydiving

...and vehicles for an astonishing entrance
- 1950s charabang
- New York taxi
- Yacht
- Harley-Davidson
- Vintage Bentley or Rolls Royce
- Classic red Cadillac

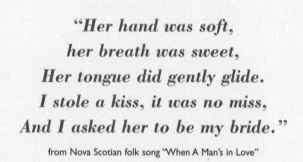

"Her hand was soft,
her breath was sweet,
Her tongue did gently glide.
I stole a kiss, it was no miss,
And I asked her to be my bride."

from Nova Scotian folk song "When A Man's in Love"

Precious Proposals

In 860 B.C. Pope Nicolas I decreed that all accepted proposals of marriage should be sealed with the giving of a gold ring, this metal being so precious the act would prevent unscrupulous suitors (and suitees) messing with holy law. The bride price in medieval Italy would often be paid in precious stones, imported as part of the trade in spices and other Eastern luxuries, and in the late fifteenth century these stones started to be set in gold and silver and given to mark the agreement of betrothal. Modern brides wear this monetary tribute on the ring finger.

The engagement ring is so important a part of the match the world over that Muslim, Hindu, and Sikh brides, who don't traditionally wear a wedding ring, sport them. Diamonds have been the stone of choice for engagement bands since the fifteenth century (worn by 70 percent of brides-to-be). Sapphire rings are second in popularity, followed by rubies and emeralds. Some couples choose a stone by the bride's birth month (see pages 20–21), others to convey intimate sentiments.

The engagement ring of the 18-year-old Danish Princess Alexandra, given in 1862, was one such "regard" or "gypsy" ring, its broad band spelling out in precious and semiprecious stones her future husband's pet name, Bertie—beryl, emerald, ruby, topaz, iacynth, emerald.

Other rings read "love" or "amour." Some grooms-in-waiting proffer a treasured heirloom piece, perhaps adapted with a more contemporary setting, but the thoughtful beau, in the knowledge that his intended has strong tastes, might opt for a "ringless proposal" followed by a shopping trip à deux…

Bridal Birthstones

Love is "more precious than emeralds and dearer than fine opals."

Oscar Wilde

The tradition of linking precious and semiprecious stones with months (and with the planets) has been traced back to the first century A.D., but the system didn't become commonly known until the eighteenth century, first in Poland, and then throughout Europe. Slightly differing stones were adopted in the Roman, Arab, Jewish, and Russian traditions.

Garnet: January's birthstone stands for constancy, fertility, and abundance, making this stone a good choice to mark a wedding.

Amethyst: February's birthstone represents sincerity, humility, and inner peace. Its violet color is associated with raised spirituality and dignity.

Carnelian or Bloodstone: These red birthstones for March are said to impart courage and self-confidence. When worn by women, the stone is reputed to protect the health of the ovaries, as is aquamarine (sign of marital harmony and a long and happy marriage), another birthstone choice this month.

Diamond: April's stone, associated with Venus, is the most rare and precious of gemstones. Brides-to-be relish the connotations it carries of indestructible love, constancy and fidelity, transparency, and purity. (For more information, see pages 12–13.)

Emerald: May's birthstone is a traditional choice for engagement rings, representing hope and success.

Pearl: June's "jewel of love" is a sign of purity and chastity. It is a good choice for lifelong matches, because it has to be worn constantly to retain the soft luster of its sheen.

Ruby: July's birthstone is a traditional choice for weddings, standing simply for love, and is said to have the power of attracting and boosting passion. The qualities of the ruby are considered most powerful when the stone is worn on the right-hand ring finger.

Sardonyx: The birthstone for August in some traditions, sardonyx is appropriate for an engagement ring because it signifies happiness in marriage. Peridot is the alternative choice this month.

Sapphire: September's stone represents wisdom and the elevation of the celestial realm. In blue, it has a calming influence.

Opal: October's birthstone represents hope and fidelity, although at points in its history it has been linked, unluckily for brides, with inconstancy.

Topaz: The birthstone for November is especially appropriate for the lifelong vows of marriage because it stands for faithfulness, good fortune, and the courage to look ahead.

Turquoise: December's stone represents harmony and good fortune. It is said to absorb impurities, ward off danger, and attract wealth.

Although I conquer all the earth,
Yet for me there is only one city.
In that city there is for
me only one house;
And in that house, one room only;
And in that room, a bed.
And one woman sleeps there,
The shining joy and jewel
of all my kingdom.

Sanskrit poem

Making a Beaded Comb

A few flowers in pale crystal shades make the perfect decoration for combs and other hair ornaments for both the bride and her attendants. Despite its delicate appearance, the finished comb is quite robust, and can easily withstand being manipulated into the most ambitious hairstyle.

MATERIALS
- *Rose wire*
- *¹/₁₀-in/2-mm rocaille beads in pale green, apricot, fuchsia, and clear glass*
- *¹/₁₆-in/1.5-mm purple glass beads*
- *Clear plastic comb*
- *White felt*

TOOLS
- *Wire cutters*
- *Flat-nosed pliers*
- *Scissors*
- *PVA (white) glue*
- *Ruler*

1 The three large flowers are each made up of five petals. For each petal, thread 46 beads onto a 12-in/30-cm length of wire.

2 Slide the first 6 beads along to 4in/10cm from the end. These will form the center of the petal. Bend the next 6in/15cm of wire into a loop and twist it to make the stalk.

3 Count off the next 8 beads. Take the wire up to the left and wrap it once around the center just above the top bead. Bring the wire down to the right and count off another 8 beads.

4 Wrap the wire once around the stalk just below the bottom bead. Make another round in the same way, with 12 beads on each side.

5 To finish off the petal, bend the center wire back behind the beads, then twist all four strands together.

6 Make four more in the same color. Hold them in a flower shape and twist the wire stalks firmly together using the pliers. Bend the petals gently into position.

7 Thread 3 beads in a different color onto a short length of wire and twist into a loop. Slip the ends of the wire between the petals, so that the beads lie in the center of the flower, and wrap them around the stalk. Make three flowers in apricot, fuchsia, and clear in this way.

8 The four leaf sprays are made from pale green beads. Thread 11 beads onto a 12-in/30-cm length of wire and slide them into the center. Pass one end of the wire through the first two beads and draw up into a loop.

9 Thread 13 beads onto one end of the wire, pass the end back through the first two beads and draw up. Make a similar loop on the other wire.

10 Thread both wires through three more beads to make a stalk. Make another two pairs of leaves, separated by a 4-bead stalk and finish off with a 5-bead stalk.

11 The three violets are made from the purple glass beads. Thread 18 beads onto an 8-in/20-cm length of wire and twist into a loop $1\frac{1}{2}$ in/4cm from one end to form a petal. Thread another 18 beads onto the long end, slide them to $\frac{1}{8}$ in/2mm from the first petal and twist into another $1\frac{1}{2}$ in/4cm loop.

12 Make another three petals in the same way, then thread on one of the rocaille beads. Pass the wire into the center of the flower behind the petals, then thread both wires through 6 green glass beads to make a stalk.

13 Hold two leaf sprays at one corner of the comb so that the stems lie along the front top edge. Cut a 6-in/15-cm length of wire and bind it tightly over the stems and in between the teeth to hold the sprays in place. Fix the other two sprays to the opposite corner. Add a flower at each end in the same way, then fix the violets to the center. Attach the third flower to fill the remaining space.

14 Flatten any sharp ends with the pliers. Cut a strip of felt to fit along the back top edge of the comb and glue it in place to cover the wire completely.

Unfortunate Coincidence

DOROTHY PARKER

By the time you swear you're his,
  Shivering and sighing,
And he vows his passion is
  Infinite, undying—
Lady, make a note of this:
  One of you is lying.

Beauty and the Beast

by

ARTHUR QUILLER COUCH

She dreamed that she was back at the Beast's palace, and wandering by a lonely path in the gardens which ended in a tangle of brushwood overhanging a cave. As she drew nearer she heard a terrible groaning, and running in haste she found the Beast stretched there on the point of death. Still in her dream she was bending over him when the stately lady stepped forth from the bushes and addressed her in a tone of grave reproach:—

"I doubt, Beauty, if even now you have come in time. Cruel, cruel of you to delay! when your delay has brought him so near to death!"

Terrified by this dream Beauty awoke in her bed with a start. "I have done wickedly!" she cried. "Am I too late? Oh, indeed I hope not!" She turned the ring upon her finger and said aloud in a firm voice: "I wish to go back to my palace and see my Beast again!"

With that she at once fell asleep, and only woke up to hear the clock chiming, "Beauty, Beauty," twelve times on the musical note she so well remembered. She was back, then, at the palace. Yes, and—oh, joy!—her faithful apes and parrots were gathered around the bed, wishing her good morning!

But none of them could tell her any news of the Beast.

They were here to serve her, and all their thoughts ended with their duty. Their good master—the lord of this splendid palace—what was he to them? At any rate nothing was to be learnt from them, and Beauty was no sooner dressed than she broke away impatiently, wandering through the house and the gardens to fill up the time until evening should bring his accustomed visit. But it was hard work filling up the time. She went into the great hall and resolutely opened the windows one by one. The shows were there as before; but opera and comedy, fête and pageant, held no meaning for her: the players were listless, the music was dull, the processions passed before her eyes but had lost their powers to amuse.

Supper-time came at length; but when after supper the minutes passed and passed and still no Beast appeared, then indeed Beauty was frightened. For a long while she waited, listened, told herself this and that, and finally in a terror rushed down into the gardens to seek for him. The alleys were dark; the bushes daunted her with their black shadows; but still up and down ran poor Beauty calling to the Beast, and calling in vain.

She was drenched with the dew, utterly lost and weary, when, after three hours, pausing for a moment's rest, she saw before her the same solitary path she had seen in her dream: and there in the moonlight she almost stumbled over the Beast.

He lay there, stretched at full length and asleep—or so she thought. So glad was she to have found him that she knelt and stroked his head, calling him by name over and over. But his flesh was cold beneath her hand, nor did he move or open his eyes.

"Ah, he is dead!" she cried, aghast.

But she put a hand over his heart, and to her inexpressible ☞

joy she felt that it was still beating. Hastily she ran to a fountain near by, and dipping water into her palms from its basin she ran and sprinkled it on his face, coaxing him with tender words as his eyes opened, and slowly—very slowly—he came to himself.

"Ah! what a fright you have given me!" she murmured. "Dear Beast, I never knew how I loved you until I feared that you were dead—yes, dead, and through my fault! But I believe, if you had died, I should have died too."

"Beauty," said the Beast faintly, "you are very good if indeed you can love such an ugly brute as I am. It is true that I was dying for you, and should have died if you had not come. I thought you had forsaken me. But are you sure?"

"Sure of what?" asked Beauty.

"That you love me?"

"Let us go back to supper," said Beauty, raising his head.

"Yes, let us go back to supper," agreed the Beast, lifting himself heavily on her arm. He still leaned on her, as they walked back to the palace together. But the supper—which they found laid for two—seemed to revive him, and in his old stupid way he asked her about the time she had spent at home, and if her father and brothers and sisters had been glad to see her.

Beauty, though weary enough after her search through the park and gardens, brisked herself up to tell of all that had happened to her in her absence. The Beast sat nodding his head and listening in his old dull way—which somehow seemed to her the most comfortable way in the world. At length he rose to go. But at the doorway he put the old blunt question,

"Beauty, will you marry me?"

"Yes, dear Beast," said Beauty; and as she said it a blaze of light filled the room. A salvo of artillery sounded, a moment later, from the park. Bang, bang! fireworks shot across the windows of the palace; sky rockets and Roman candles exploded and a magnificent set-piece wrote across the darkness in letters of fire—"LONG LIVE BEAUTY AND THE BEAST!"

Beauty turned to ask what all these rejoicings might mean; and, with that, she gave a cry. The Beast had vanished, and in his place stood the beloved Prince of her dreams! He smiled and stretched out his hands to her. Scarcely knowing what she did, she was stretching hers, to take them, when above the banging of fireworks in the avenues there sounded a rolling of wheels. It drew to the porch, and presently there entered the stately lady she had seen in her dreams. It was the very same; and, all astounded as she was, Beauty did reverence to her.

But the stately lady was as eager to do reverence to Beauty. "Best and dearest," said she, "my son is going to love you always; as how should he not, seeing that by your courage you have rescued him from the enchantment under which he has lain so long, and have restored him to his natural form? But suffer also his mother, a Queen, to bless you!"

Beauty turned again to her lover and saw that he, who had been a Beast, was indeed the Prince of her dreams and handsomer than the day. So they were married and lived happy ever after; nay, so happy were they that all over the world folks told one another and set down in writing this wonderful history of Beauty and the Beast.

> *"Look down you gods,*
> *And on this couple*
> *Drop a blessed crown!"*
>
> from *The Tempest* by William Shakespeare

The Language of Flowers

Concocted in Europe during the eighteenth and nineteenth centuries, the language of flowers comprised a pick-and-mix selection of folk beliefs drawn from many global traditions. Some commentators trace its roots to the *selam*, a Turkish love letter in the form of a bouquet of flowers. Others counter that this was a widely reported misinterpretation by the romantically-minded wife of an English ambassador sent to Turkey in 1717. Whatever its origins, the language of flowers was popularized across Europe by a tranche of French books on the subject from the early nineteenth century onward, and the often diverse meanings were soon in such common usage that "*durch die Blume sprechen*" passed into parlance. Florists and brides today still enjoy toying with the most long-lasting of the romantic meanings attached to flowers, although much of the subtlety and grammar of the tradition is lost on us. At one time lovers could exchange (in theory at least) complex coded messages via bouquets, the very placement of each flower in the bunch carrying significance. And it wasn't just the blooms that mattered. Whether thorns and foliage were removed or kept intact sent different messages, and the number of berries or leaves could evoke tears of joy or grief.

Pin Money

Across the traditions guests equip the home of a new couple by donating cash, and the act of giving is the prompt for a great deal of merrymaking. Hungarian men offer the bride coins in exchange for a kiss (of late women do the same to the groom). The Polish tradition has young men pin notes to the bride's dress in exchange for a dance at the wedding feast (and here too, women advance on the new husband). The collection point is a little more sedate in other traditions, the bride sitting in waiting with a shawl, apron, or even a sieve in Finland to catch the coins. In Italy, the bride carries a special satin bag in which to collect *buste*, donation envelopes. Sometimes an attendant helps out: in Switzerland a godmother or *gelbe frau* distributes red handkerchiefs to guests to be filled with money and returned to the bride. Couples in the U.K. and U.S. with no such family traditions have been known to employ a dressmaker's form for less touchy-feely donations toward a bed- or baby-fund.

Gift ideas for the couple who already have everything:

- Donations toward a piece of art, around the world flight tickets, trip on the Orient Express
- Pledges to charity
- Case of good wine or whisky
- Hire of matching Harley-Davidsons or a yacht for a weekend
- Plant part of a woodland
- Star named after the couple

Pillar of Salt

Like the kiss that seals wedding rituals, salt was used in the past to ratify an agreement, and so it's no surprise that this life-sustaining substance is represented at many marriage ceremonies. Russian newlyweds are invited to partake of bread and a little salt at the start of the wedding feast. Like the salt tasted with the Friday loaf on the Jewish Sabbath, it is a sign to remember God's covenant to man. The shoes of German brides are scattered with the stuff, and they are urged to carry salt and bread with them to the nuptial rites to ensure abundance in their future home. In France this guards against infertility, for salt, like everything from the sea, is considered an aphrodisiac. It also preserves, of course, and so carries intimations of immortality, or a long-lived, ever-steady match. Because empires have been built on salt revenue, having a portable store of it on your wedding day has good implications for your future prosperity.

And the protection from spoiling salt extends to foodstuffs, ballooning around the bride and groom to ward off the evil eye that seems to haunt the betrothed as it does newborns. Salt blesses, preserves, and protects the union.

Pearls of Love

A single strand of pearls is the traditional wedding day jewelry choice for many brides. It exudes understated class and the effortless grace of such role-model brides as Grace Kelly and Jackie Kennedy. If the pearls are not a passed-on family piece, they might be donated by the groom, a custom in Europe. An Indian man seeking a match might offer the father of his dream bride a pearl ring, which the father bequeaths to the daughter once the alliance is agreed. Pearls are the semiprecious stones most often used to emphasize purity and constancy. Wearing them is said to bring about a similarly pure, peaceful love. Pearls are the stones ruled by the moon, the planet most associated with women and the constant flux of the menstrual cycle, and in India a symbol of romance in itself. Pearls are also entwined in love myths: the Greek goddess of love and beauty Aphrodite, meaning "born from the foam," and her Roman alter ego Venus emerged from the ocean, like a pearl, in a scallop shell. In the islands of the South Pacific, the bride price comprises strings of beads of coral and shell, dolphin and porpoise teeth. For centuries used for trading, these beads have considerable value and are a way of passing wealth from family to family. The more finely wrought shell jewelry the bride wears, the better the indication of her status. North American Indian brides too displayed wealth with headdresses of coveted shells, such as the *dentalium* worn by Yakima Indian brides of the Pacific Northwest.

Something Old, Something New

Perhaps the most well-known bridal dress tradition still adhered to is set out in the nineteenth-century rhyme that states the essentials every bride needs to include in her outfit to bring about a long and happy match:

> *"Something old, something new*
> *Something borrowed, something blue*
> *And a silver sixpence in your shoe."*
> Nineteenth-century rhyme

Something old

In the days when a bride left her family never to return home, carrying something old with her would have offered a poignant reminder of her girlhood and family customs. With her dowry trunk, it would have been immensely reassuring, becoming a treasured piece within the new family to pass on to her own daughters. Some brides in the past carried a handkerchief embroidered with their maiden name initials, perhaps cut from a particularly treasured girlhood gown as "something old." Others wore an heirloom lace veil, a single strand of family pearls or other piece of good jewelry, a treasured tiara or fine wax headdress.

Something new

Brides *in memoriam* have strived to have an entirely new outfit on their wedding day, as if to cast aside everything that defined their unmarried state. Above all, the dress would have to be fresh; more often today, with vintage fashions popular, it's a fabulous pair of shoes. Queen Victoria set a trend by yearning for something "new but made to resemble old," achieving this with a gown made of folksy-looking handmade lace.

Something borrowed

Being lent something to wear on your wedding day by a woman in a long-lived and happy marriage is a means of transferring a little accrued happiness. Heirloom lace veils were in the past the item most commonly borrowed by brides—perhaps because of their exorbitant cost. Still today an antique Cathedral-length veil will outprice many a wedding dress beneath it. Most of these exquisite, gossamer-thin creations were hand-pieced in the nineteenth century, when the craze for veils was at its height, and lace adorned everything that stood still: beds and armchairs, shelves and mantelpieces, pitchers and trays. Such lace has an ivory sheen from age that imparts a golden haze no modern veil can duplicate. Borrowing a wedding dress from a much-loved aunt or mother, and having it altered to fit you and current runway trends is another option for borrowed luck (especially if the original owner was married during a golden time for fashion, such as the 1920s or 1950s). But bear in mind the motto that borrowing a dress brings good fortune to the wearer but bad luck to the lender. Some commentators say the borrowed item should be of gold, betokening prosperity to come. ☞

Something blue

Blue is the color of the heavenly realm and links the bride with all things spiritual. In the Christian tradition, it is the color most often associated with the Virgin Mary's robes, and so to wear a little blue annexes to each bride the virtues of Christ's mother: fidelity, devotion, and unquestioning faith. Some sources trace the blue element of the rhyme further back, to ancient Israel. In Numbers 15:38, God commands people to weave a blue thread into the fringes of clothing as a constant reminder to heed his commandments. Blue threads appear for this reason on the Jewish *tallit*, or prayer shawl. And so adding a blue thread to everyday clothes elevates them from the secular world and transforms them into a spiritual garment suitable for prayer and sacred sacraments such as marriage. Some traditions say you should keep your piece of blue to pass on to your daughter.

Ways to avoid the ubiquitous blue garter

- Stitch blue ribbon or thread into the hem
- Wear topaz or sapphire earrings—in India wearing earrings on your wedding day ensures your marriage will always be happy
- Buy those blue Manolos you've always coveted
- Get a meaningful tattoo where only your husband will see it
- Include flowering rosemary, forget-me-nots, or hyacinths in your bouquet or circlet, according to the season

...and a sixpence in your shoe

A Swedish bride embarking on her journey to the marriage venue places a silver coin donated by her father in her left shoe, and a gold coin given by her mother in her right shoe, a sign that she will never run short. American brides make it a penny, which might be stuck to the sole for comfort.

A Spanish bride is ritually offered 13 coins, known as *monedas* or *arras*, by her future spouse. The sum represents a nominal price paid for the bride, given now not to her father but to the woman herself. She carries these tokens to church not in her shoe, but in a silk purse, since originally they were blessed during the service. In France the same coins are known as the *treizain*. The 13 pieces of gold and silver act as a folk spell to bring lasting prosperity to the new home, while also representing the groom's vow to care for the bride by sharing with her all his worldly goods. The old Catholic marriage service states that the bridegroom should offer gold and silver coins alongside the rings for a blessing, and when placing the ring on his bride's finger declare, "With this ring I thee wed; this gold and silver I thee give, with my body I thee worship and with all my worldly goods I thee endow."

Married when the year is new,
he'll be loving, kind and true,
When February birds do sing,
cherish you your wedding ring.
If you wed when March winds blow,
joy and sorrow both you'll know.
Marry in April if you can,
thus joy for maiden and for man.
Marry in the month of May,
and you will never rue the day.
Marry when June roses grow,
over hills and far you'll go.
Those who in July do wed,
must labor hard for daily bread.
Whoever wed in August be,
many a fortune is sure to see.
Marry in September's shrine,
your living will be rich and fine.
If in October you do marry,
love will come but riches tarry.
If you wed in bleak November,
only joys will come, remember.
When December snows fall fast,
marry and true love will last.

Traditional English rhyme

Good-Luck Charms

"Parents can give a dowry but not luck."
Yiddish saying

For nineteenth-century American home weddings, the couple would stand beneath a good luck sign such as a dove or wishbone to take their vows, in a merging of the sacred and secular. Though we might claim it's all mumbo jumbo, modern brides still cling to superstitions on their wedding day to ensure good fortune—being showered with paper horseshoes and bells, tossing the bouquet, and driving away in a car decorated with shoes and tin cans. If you don't want to go as far as carrying a decorative horseshoe or chimney sweeper, a charm bracelet makes a pretty addition to a wedding outfit, echoing the waist decorations strung with lucky symbols of Ancient Egyptian and Brazilian brides.

- *Horseshoe:* A crescent shape attracts or "draws" good fortune; with the points (heel) uppermost, it catches and stores good luck. Iron holds the power to deflect the evil eye.

- *Shamrock:* Associated with the Irish wedding toast. "For each petal on the shamrock, this brings a wish your way: Good health, good luck, and happiness for today and every day."

- **Shoe:** Carrying a loved one's shoe near your heart or hanging it over your bed is said to command power over the beloved. Used shoes are thrown after a bride to wish her luck on her journey, it being considered extra fortuitous if they hit her or lodge on the car or carriage.

- **Chimney sweep, ladder, or brush:** Stand for the good luck afforded by the sanctuary of hearth and home.

- **Bells:** The joyous peal of bells that sounds after a church wedding is thought to scare away spirits intent on mischief and warn of evil approaching.

- **Fish or frog:** Fertility symbols.

- **Heart shapes:** Engraved with initials they bless specific individuals; twin hearts pierced by a single arrow denote reciprocated love.

- **Wishing well:** Brings good luck in money matters.

- **Four-leaf clover:** A luck charm especially associated with weddings, each of the leaves said to offer wealth, fame, love, and good health. ☞

- **Key:** Denotes success in the arts of love and wisdom, offers access to another world, unlocks the heart, and is a sign of a new household.

- **Grapes or twining vines:** Stand for abundance and fecundity.

- **Coin:** Symbolic and actual wealth, as in the coin necklaces and belts that formed part of a girl's dowry in the Middle East.

- **Pomegranate:** Ancient Greek symbol of fertility carried by goddess of marriage Hera; worn by newly wed brides in ancient Rome to signify their status.

- **Peony, peach, and shou symbols:** Denote marital harmony in China.

- **Chinese he-he gods:** Statues of the twin gods of prosperity are a sign of harmony in marriage.

- **Love birds:** Two magpies, doves, swallows, or butterflies are Chinese symbols of wedded bliss (as is a duck or kingfisher).

- **Umbrella or parasol:** A Finnish charm to shield the wearer from misfortune.

"*Monday for health,*
Tuesday for wealth,
Wednesday the best day of all;
Thursday for losses,
Friday for crosses
Saturday no luck at all."

English rhyme to choose a lucky wedding day

Light of My Life

"When two people are at one in their inmost hearts
They shatter even the strength of iron or of bronze
And when two people understand each other in their inmost hearts
Their worlds are sweet and strong like the fragrance of orchids "

from the *I Ching*

Male and female, light and dark, yin and yang converge in a wedding, dualities reconciled for a moment. The coming together not just of two people, but two families, sets of traditions, and ways of being gives every newlywed couple the freedom to break boundaries and start fresh. The Japanese wedding couple performs a ritual that embodies this beautifully. On entering the feasting room after the marriage ceremony, where all the guests are seated, bride and groom make for their own parents' tables. At these separate tables, they each light a tall, thin candle from fatter candles sitting in front of their Mom and Dad. The bridal couple then pass through the dining room, lighting candles set at each of the guest tables until they meet at the front and together light a huge "wedding candle" on the table where they will sit together as man and wife. The light of life from two separate sources is finally burning in one flame.

Right: A Russian marriage ceremony where the bride and groom are each given a burning candle before they exchange rings.

Jumping the Broom

Trial marriages aren't a new idea. Woodland weddings, as they were known in medieval England, traditionally took place during May Day celebrations, a raucous time of courting and coupling that occurred during the old Celtic festival of Beltane at the beginning of May. The carousing celebrated the coming again of the sun and the beginning of summer, season of light (the term *Bel* is associated with the ancient sun god in many cultures, while *tan* is a Celtic word for fire). Partners held a ceremony with friends, pledging to marry for a year and a day, and leaping over a fire (or a broom, representing hearth and home) while holding hands. This trial period could be declared null if either party considered it so after the allotted time. Trial marriages were also common at Lammas, season of harvest and end of the Celtic year, starting on August 1. It was marked with festivities, feasting, and hiring fairs that brought together single men and women from miles around and featured circle dancing. Couples got together for the length of a Lammas fair, giving rise to the term, "Lammas marriages." Modern Wiccans hold handfasting ceremonies during which a couple choose how long to set their partnership: a year and a day perhaps, or "till death us do part." Some couples jump a broom as a symbol of their new status as householders. This ritual is also being reclaimed by African Americans as a symbolic rite to honor the history of Africans living in slavery in the Americas when they were prevented from engaging in their own marriage traditions.

Left: Disaster strikes when a bride jumps over a fire to secure happiness in her marriage.

The Trousseau

"Shantung is a real hard-wearing all-silk material. It is ideal for everyday wear in winter and summer. It washes perfectly and will last for years. When planning a trousseau do not forget to include it."

from *Pictorial Dressmaking*, 1940

The hope chest, the bottom drawer, the dowry trunk—all bring to mind the heart-fluttering longing of young girls for a future life filled with love, happiness, and fulfilment. In the past, the trousseau has embodied the ambition, expectations, and pride of her family, too. The bride's trousseau—the term derives from a diminutive form of the French word *trousse* or bundle—once comprised everything a young woman would require for her wedding, to set up a family home, and to do duty as "underwear" for life. It would contain the bridal dress, a brand new going-away dress, and gowns suitable for every occasion one might encounter during the honeymoon— balls and afternoon parties, tennis and croquet, yachting and travel, breakfasts and tea dances. Alongside the toiletries and cosmetics, cutlery and dinner service, there would, in earlier years, be beautifully worked linen. A young woman was expected to bring with her to a marriage a complete set of sheets, towels, and tableware as well as more personal pieces, including nightdresses, monogrammed handkerchiefs, petticoats, camisoles, stockings, and other lingerie, set with lace and adorned with embroidery and drawn thread work. The trousseau provided a showcase for a girl's needlework skills—and those of her aunts, mother, and sisters, for all might contribute. Wealthy families would employ the best seamstresses they could in order to supplement the daughter's work, although by 1880 mail-order catalogues such as Bloomingdales were offering American brides-to-be cut-price trousseau sets that included everything from nightgowns to walking dresses. Home-worked pieces formed a very visible sign of a family's wealth and social standing, and in parts of the world, this tradition lingers. In the mountains of Romania on June 29 the annual festival of the trousseau is celebrated, and families put their intricately worked handicrafts on display. The trousseaux of society brides have raised such public interest in the past that they have been speculated on in fashion magazines and newspapers. On December 15, 1877, *Harper's Bazaar* carried the story of the famed Miss Vanderbilt's trousseau, writing, "The elegant trousseau prepared for Miss Vanderbilt has claimed so much public notice of late that we have taken special pains to lay the details of it before our readers, who may be glad to profit by the useful suggestions afforded by so many tasteful toilettes." At a time of burgeoning "new money" it was considered fashionable to air your wares in public. Thirty years' on, to be so exhibitionist as to put your smalls on show revealed only a lack of refinement.

"Mademoiselle Rouault was busy with her trousseau. Part of it was ordered from Rouen; her night-dresses and night-caps she made herself, from patterns lent her by friends."

from *Madame Bovary* by Gustave Flaubert

The Tales of Chekhov

by

ANTON CHEKHOV

Soon afterward the door opened and I saw a tall, thin girl of nineteen, in a long muslin dress with a gilt belt from which, I remember, hung a mother-of-pearl fan. She came in, dropped a curtsy, and flushed crimson. Her long nose, which was slightly pitted with smallpox, turned red first, and then the flush passed up to her eyes and her forehead.

"My daughter," chanted the little lady, "and, Manetchka, this is a young gentleman who has come," etc.

I was introduced, and expressed my surprise at the number of paper patterns. Mother and daughter dropped their eyes.

"We had a fair here at Ascension," said the mother, "we always buy materials at the fair, and then it keeps us busy with sewing till the next year's fair comes round again. We never put things out to be made. My husband's pay is not very ample, and we are not able to permit ourselves luxuries. So we have to make up everything ourselves."

"But who will ever wear such a number of things? There are only two of you?"

"Oh…as though we were thinking of wearing them! They are not to be worn; they are for the trousseau!"

"Ah, *maman*, what are you saying?" said the daughter, and she crimsoned again. "Our visitor might suppose it was true. I don't intend to get married. Never!"

She said this, but at the very word "married" her eyes glowed….Manetchka threw off her shyness for a moment and showed me the tobacco-pouch she was embroidering for her father. When I pretended to be greatly struck by her work, she flushed crimson and whispered something in her mother's ear. The latter beamed all over, and invited me to go with her to the storeroom. There I was shown five large trunks, and a number of smaller trunks and boxes.

"This is her trousseau," her mother whispered, "we made it all ourselves."

The Hope Chest

"To keep linen white in a trunk, wrap it in blue paper and place blue paper between the folds."

from *The Home Encyclopedia*, 1956

The traditional cedarwood chest in which the trousseau was packed often became a family heirloom, passed on from mother to daughter, a store of memories as well as precious objects. The wood of the cedar tree is a symbol of constant faith and longevity, used as incense and in temple building across the ancient world. Its smoky, dry scent is reputed to calm nervous tension, bring about composure, and focus the mind in the here and now, all properties useful for anxious brides-to-be. Cedar chests are still handcrafted in the old manner across the United States, coming to rest in newlyweds' homes as blanket storage or coffee tables until a daughter is old enough to start collecting items for her own trousseau. In regions of India, parents of the bride would donate an ornately embellished wooden chest in which to keep her trousseau. It was carved with traditional motifs for luck and fertility, abundance, and desire: stylized flowers and ornate creeping foliage, parrots and peacocks, mango leaves and coconuts, and, of course, the erotic conch shell.

The first wedding to take place in the White House, in 1886, of President Grover Cleveland to Frances Folsom.

The Meaning of Flowers

Nineteenth-century brides were urged to base their floral arrangements—wreath, bouquet, displays for church and home, groom's boutonnière—around one bloom which had special significance to them in the grammar of flowers or spoke of family connections. This then would become their flower for life, and they would expect a bouquet of the blooms on each anniversary to come. Here are some flowers considered suitable in the language of flowers for a wedding.

Almond blossom: a lover's charm

Amaryllis: pride; splendid beauty

Anemone: unfading love; sincerity

Aster: herb of Venus, said by the Latin poet Virgil to litter the altars of the gods; in China, fidelity

Carnation: sign of marriage in China
- white: pure love
- pink: never forgotten; undying love
- red: "my heart aches for you"
- solid color: "yes"

Chrysanthemum: token of eternity in China and Japan

- red: "I love you"
- white: truthfulness

Cornflower: delicacy

Dahlia: elegance

Daisy: innocence; "you have as many virtues as petals on this flower"

Forget-me-not: yearning; desperate love

Freesia: trusting innocence

Gardenia: secret love

Gladiolus: love at first sight

Heather: in Scotland used for wedding mattresses
- pink: good luck
- white: protection
- lavender: admiration

Honeysuckle: devoted love; generosity

Hyacinth: flower of beloved

friendship in ancient Greece
- blue: constancy
- white: loveliness
- pink: playful joy

Ivy: fidelity; wedded love
Jasmine: India's bridal flower
- yellow: grace and elegance
- white: friendship

Lavender: devotion
Lilac: flower of springtime celebrations
- purple: first love
- white: youthful innocence

Lily: purity and chastity
- calla: magnificent beauty
- tiger: prosperity

Lily-of-the-valley: constancy; humility; new life; return of happiness (and so suited to second marriages)
Love-in-a-mist: complexity
Mimosa: secret love
Narcissus: stay sweet
Orange blossom: eternal love
Orchid: refined love; in China, perfection
Pansy: remembrance; the flower of St. Valentine; all white until Cupid fired his arrow and endowed a myriad of colors
Peach blossom: "I am your captive"
Peony: married love and fertility in China
Periwinkle: sweet remembrance
Pink: pure affection
Ranunculus: "I am dazzled by your charm"
Snowdrop: hope
Stock: lasting beauty
Sunflower: loyalty; splendor; blind infatuation
- dwarf: adoration

Sweetpea: blissful pleasure
Sweet William: "give me a smile"
Tulip: violent love in its native Turkey
- red: love declared; on fire with love
- yellow: "I love your sunny smile"
- variegated: "you have beautiful eyes"

Violet: faithfulness, modesty; a plant governed by Venus

Love's Philosophy

PERCY BYSSHE SHELLEY

The fountains mingle with the river
and the rivers with the ocean,
The winds of Heaven mix for ever
With a sweet emotion;
Nothing in the world is single
All things by a law divine
In one spirit meet and mingle
Why not I with thine?

See the mountains kiss high Heaven
And the waves clasp one another;
No sister-flower would be forgiven
If it disdained its brother;
And the sunlight clasps the earth
And the moonbeams kiss the sea:
What is all this sweet work worth
If thou kiss not me?

Crystallizing Rose Petals

This is the classic wedding cake adornment. Use roses from your own garden that you can guarantee are pesticide-free. Petals which are slightly past their prime have the best aroma and taste. This method also works well with violets.

ingredients
rose petals
2 eggs
bag superfine sugar

1 Prepare each petal by cutting away the bitter white "heel" at the base. Wash the petals and pat dry carefully.

2 Separate the eggs. Place the whites in a mixing bowl and beat gently with an egg whisk until frothy but not stiff.

3 Using a sieve, sift a layer of sugar onto a wide, shallow dish.

4 Using a fine paintbrush, paint each petal with the egg white.

5 Gently rest the petal on the sugar, then flip to coat the other side.

6 Leave to dry on a metal cooling rack. Repeat until all the petals are covered, whisking more egg whites and adding another layer of sugar as necessary.

Herbal Lore for Bouquets

Swedish brides and their attendants used to carry a huge posy of weeds and distinctly rotten-smelling herbs to ward off trolls said to be attracted by wedding parties to cause mischief. More palatable herbs regularly turn up in the traditional fresh flower circlet, which the Victorians moved from the head to be carried by hand. Many of them are evergreens—potent symbols of long-lasting fidelity—and a good few are sacred to Venus.

Rosemary: Embodying commitment and lasting love (touching the groom with a sprig apparently guarantees his fidelity), sprigs of this herb are traditional in bridal headbands and bouquets. The resinous scent of rosemary stimulates the memory, becoming an emblem of remembrance, and so of love and friendship.

Yarrow: Girls might place a sprig of this plant, ruled by Venus, beneath the pillow in order to dream of love. Planting a piece from the bridal bouquet outside the home of a newly married couple is said to ensure seven years' fidelity (it should be renewed every seven years).

Myrtle: The flower most traditional in English bridal bouquets, used since medieval times to bring about fortune, peace, and long life. A famed aphrodisiac, the plant is sacred to Venus and Hathor, Egyptian goddess of love and beauty, and is a Hebrew emblem of marriage. Arabic lore holds that Adam was sent out of the Garden of Eden with a branch of myrtle picked from the bower in which he first spoke his love for Eve.

Sage: Deemed appropriate for wedding bouquets because it symbolizes domesticity, wisdom, and longevity. In early summer the lilac flowers make an aromatic addition to bridal headdresses, having a clean fragrance that calms while quickening the senses.

Hawthorn Blossom: Carrying a sprig of this plant ensures newlyweds happiness and prosperity across Europe. In a bridal bouquet it links the carrier with the virtues of the Virgin Mary, to whom it has been considered sacred at times, especially in Italy.

White Heather: Some say every Scottish bride should carry a sprig of white heather; it even shows up here as a symbol of good luck atop the wedding cake. One might wash down the cake with heather ale, a recently revived staple drink from the Highlands. Heather was a mattress plant in Scotland, and many a bridal bed would have been fragrant with its honey-scented flowers. A spray placed beneath the bed brings luck.

Ivy: First included in a bridal bouquet by Queen Victoria, who wore a wreath of Osborne ivy, from her home on the Isle of Wight, interwoven with diamonds. Ivy is deemed a feminine plant (to holly's prickly masculinity). As an evergreen, it connotes eternal life, and the manner in which its tendrils climb and cling, seemingly smothering other plants, was suggestive to Victorians of all-conquering love and a successful relationship's drive for constant growth. Late flowering, ivy might be considered a symbol of life when everything else is dying. Ivy leaves were once used for love divination.

My True Love Hath My Heart

SIR PHILIP SIDNEY

My true love hath my heart and I have his,
  By just exchange, one for another given;
I hold him dear, and mine he cannot miss;

Above: *Wedding Procession*, by Maurice Denis

There never was a better bargain driven.
My heart in me keeps him and me in one;
My heart in him his thoughts and senses guides;
He loves my heart for once it was his own;
I cherish him, because in me it bides.
My true love hath my heart and I have his.

Spring Floral Displays

- Pot up white hyacinth bulbs in white pudding bowls for their dusky scent.
- Plant small galvanized buckets with snowdrop bulbs.
- Grow hyacinth bulbs in tall glass tanks of water.
- Paint a wooden box white and plant with allium globes on tall stems. Cover the soil with white gravel.
- Sprout paper-white narcissus bulbs from antique terracotta plant pots or white enamel buckets. The intense aroma can fill a marquee.
- Mass tulips of one shade—shocking pink or elegant midnight perhaps—in coordinated colored vases.
- Fill rustic pitchers with scented lilac.
- Wrap pots of tiny narcissus in contrasting-colored tissue paper: let guests take them home as party favors.
- Line woven baskets with gingham and pile high with tiny chocolate eggs.
- Plant up pots of pansies and violas tied with wide organza ribbon.
- Stand tall white enamel pitchers of pussy willow or catkins on the floor.
- Pin branches of cherry blossom over the entrances to a marquee.
- Use lengths of flowering broom in tall vessels.
- Float camellia heads in wide glass bowls filled with water.
- Plant ornamental cabbages in galvanized pots.
- Too early in the season for the blooms you want? Opt instead for bright garlands of tissue flowers like the ones used at Indian weddings.

Spring Flowers for Bouquets

Freesias: This traditional choice comes in various pastel colors to suit every shade of white gown: yellow and cream smell sweetest.

Mimosa: Sweet-scented fluffy yellow balls with a whimsical air.

Lily-of-the-Valley: The tiny white bells with their lush foliage and heady fragrance are traditional at Christian weddings, since the flower is linked with the Virgin Mary. Her tears at the Crucifixion were said to have sprouted into this flower.

Tulips: Fringed varieties have a crinkly edged glamour, while the beautiful "broken" or streaked tulips have started wars and bankrupted states. In their native Turkey, tulips are said to have sprung from the tears of the unrequited lover, Ferhad.

Hyacinths: Swooning with scent; delicate varieties such as grape hyacinth are perfect for a bouquet.

Alliums: Frothy balloon-like heads that suit a modern theme.

Lilac: Beautiful floral turrets in colors from mauve to cream.

Pinks: Old-fashioned clove-scented dianthus signified an engagement in the medieval iconography of painting, and varieties are still named for the intended of the grower, or have names such as "Bridal Veil." Look for lacy or fringed-edged varieties in colors ranging from blush pink to deep raspberry.

Sweet Williams: Another stunner from the dianthus family, with raspberry ripple stripes and frilly foliage.

Ranunculus: Full-bodied voluptuous blooms with copious petals suggesting fecundity and lazy sensuality.

Divination to Find a Husband

*"O good Saint Faith, be kind tonight
And bring to me my heart's delight;
Let my future husband view
And be my vision chaste and true."*

English folk spell

If you sleep with a piece of the rich fruity wedding cake (representing the groom) and its icing (the bride) beneath your pillow, you will dream of your husband to be, goes the tale. In fact there seem to be numerous ways to divine your future spouse. Here are some tried-and-tested customs for auspicious days of the year, which tend to be nights before Saints days. Other key times for hopeful lovers' divination charms are Halloween, Christmas, and New Year's Eve.

January 20, St. Agnes' Eve: Focusing your mind on your intention, pick pins from a pincushion and pin them onto your sleeve. Sleep with your hands behind your head to dream of your future husband.

April 24, St. Mark's Eve: Just before midnight mix together an eggshell each of salt, flour, and barley meal, moisten with water to make a dough, then bake and eat to dream of your partner-to-be. Or sit in front of a mirror by the light of a single dim candle and repeat the following words to see his shadow in the glass, "Come lover, come lad and make my heart glad; For husband I'll have you for good or for bad."

October 6, St. Faith's Day: Bake a cake, turning it nine times in the oven during the baking period. Cut into twenty-seven slices, and divide among your girlfriends. Pass a slice through the wedding ring of a happily married woman, asking St. Faith to reveal your future husband in a dream.

November 25 St. Catherine's Day: Place a wreath of greenery on a statue of St. Catherine, asking to receive a vision of your partner.

December 20 St. Thomas' Eve: Set a sprig of evergreen beneath your pillow for dreams of your intended. Or write each letter of the alphabet on a separate piece of paper and float them in a basin of water, placing it beneath your bed. In the morning your lover's initials will still be floating.

Other traditions

- Place two chestnuts or hazelnuts in an open fire, naming them after yourself and an admirer. If they burst, forget your dreams. If they glow brightly, so will your passion.
- Peel an apple, keeping the curl of peel whole, and cast it over your left shoulder. The initial it resembles will be that of your true love.
- Pull out a hair and thread a ring onto it. Tie the ends to your ring finger. Hold your palm over a pitcher so the ring dangles down. Allow it to set up its own swinging motion; it will strike the pitcher as many times as there are years until your marriage.

Love Divination Rhyme for Daisy Petals

One I love,
Two I love,
Three I love, I say,
Four I love with all my heart,
Five I cast away;
Six he loves me,
Seven he don't,
Eight we're lovers both;
Nine he comes,
Ten he tarries,
Eleven he courts,
Twelve he marries.

Designed by
Helen Rose

Fairytale Weddings

When 26-year-old Hollywood princess Grace Kelly married
real life Prince Rainier of Monaco in April 1954, the match
was declared the wedding of the century. The movie star's
gown, seen by some 30 million TV viewers in nine countries,
inspired a wave of copies, a tribute to the dressmaking vision
and design of Helen Rose, the head costume designer at
MGM studios. The fitted style with stand-up collar, long
sleeves, and a bustled, gathered bell skirt (its foundation, three
petticoats of silk and taffeta) topped with a Juliet cap covered
in seed pearls remains essential inspiration for demure brides
today (see it on display in the bride's hometown of
Philadelphia, at the Philadelphia Museum of Art).

The dress set a bridal trend away from floaty fabrics toward
opulent gowns made in weighty materials richly adorned: it was
cut from 300 yards of Valenciennes lace, 25 yards of silk
taffeta, and the same amount of peau de soie, while the 125-
year-old veil of silk tulle and Brussels rosepoint lace was
embroidered with 1,000 tiny pearls. The bride carried a
bouquet of lily-of-the-valley, which became the flower of the
season, and her husband flamboyantly cut the cake with the
ceremonial sword that decorated his military uniform. MGM
bought the rights to the wedding, and fans can track it down
on video. Alternatively, watch *High Society*. Based on the run-
up to a society wedding, this classic movie starring Grace Kelly
was made as she prepared for her own marriage and shows off
her groomed grace and cool chic to perfection.

Princess Elizabeth gets fitted for her wedding gown, 1947

The Rationed Bride

When clothes rationing was introduced into wartime Britain in May 1941 to make space in factories for the manufacture of munitions, and all silk and cotton was going into the construction of parachutes and kitbags, *Vogue* declared that now only brides and newborns would get a new wardrobe. Each person was issued with 66 coupons a year, reduced to just 41 by 1945 (11 coupons were required for a regular dress). Even brides were urged to "make do and mend," and innovative young women altered existing dresses and constructed outfits from furnishing fabric and curtains, many preferring an everyday dress for their wedding that could be worn time and again to a less practical, single-occasion robe. Manmade rayon satin, in the U.S. sold as "artificial silk" and aimed at the bridal market, was embraced enthusiastically, not just as a sign of working toward the war effort, but because it hung so beautifully.

Princess (soon to be Queen) Elizabeth's wedding in 1947 to Prince Philip was a rationing wedding: she was allotted just 100 coupons to play with. Royal dress designer Norman Hartnell based her ivory silk dress on a clinging gown he spotted in a Botticelli painting, and its sweetheart neckline, tight-fitting bodice, and A-line skirt set trends. Some 20,000 seed pearls were ordered from the U.S. for the ornate embellishments on dress and train: trails of jasmine and garlands of orange blossom, the white rose of York, and wheat ears, a traditional motif for English wedding dresses because of its association with fertility, and also a patriotic nod to the millions of householders "digging for victory" in their own backyards. Silkworms for the Scottish-woven silk were sourced from friendly China rather than the regular silkworm breeding axis nations of Italy and Japan. She borrowed a diamond tiara made in 1919 in Russia (another vital ally nation) for Queen Mary that doubled as a necklace once detached from its frame. Thousands of copies were made throughout the second half of the 20th century.

In France, women's special-occasion wear for weddings and other festivities got ever more extravagant and frivolous. Every visible meter of expensive fabric, excessive trimmings, conspicuous color, and deluxe decoration was a slap in the face to the occupying German army's effort to conserve scant resources and conscript fashion and fabric workers into Hitler's war effort. After the war, the reconstruction of the textile industry in France sent patriotic brides in the U.S., France, and Britain into a frenzy for French lace from cities such as Chantilly and Lyon. Lace at weddings had been popularized by Princess Elizabeth's gown and the emergence of the "New Elizabethan" styles that marked the beginning of her reign and the end of rationing in 1949.

Princess Elizabeth's wedding gown,
designed by Norman Hartnell

Princess Diana's wedding
gown, designed by
Elizabeth Emanuel

Welsh Love Spoons

Finding two spoons in your saucer is still held in parts of Britain to presage a wedding, but it's in Wales that spoons and love are serious business. As early as 1600, young men would carve love spoons for a sweetheart in the prelude to courtship, taking up to a month to gauge a pattern of intricate interconnecting symbols from a single lump of wood. If the woman accepted the spoon, a date was set for the marriage.

Sycamore, a pale fine-grained timber, was the first choice for these spoons. A favorite of turners and kitchen cabinet makers, it can be carved in the green and is judged the best wood for bread boards and other cooking utensils since it doesn't taint food. Sycamore holds a symbolic charge, too. Because the sycamore is one of the first trees to show buds of green in spring, it is associated with fertility and springtime matchmaking rituals, being brought home to decorate the house on May day, and used to carve Jack O' Lent or Jack in the Green figures. The elongated handle of each love spoon would differ, but a well-established grammar of symbols enabled the intended to read its encoded messages. As well as the obvious intertwined hearts, bells and horseshoes, and vines and stylized flowers, Celtic crosses and knotwork designs were popular. Sailing and farming motifs made an appearance, too. Carving spoons kept sailors busy for weeks at sea and occupied a farm worker's winter evenings, just as young men stuck indoors on long dark nights in Sweden would carve imaginatively decorated wooden cookie moulds for their sweethearts. The more intricate and imaginative the spoon, the more vivid the outpouring of affection, with piercing and fretwork deemed especially impressive. The single piece of wood might be transformed into a chain of links, a moveable ball in a cage (a sign not of imprisonment but of protective love), or even emerge into two or three bowls (representing the couple and baby). Love spoons remain a popular way for couples with Celtic roots to mark an engagement, wedding, or birth, and are often engraved with names and dates.

Grammar of symbols

- Celtic knotwork: love without beginning or end
- Celtic cross: "my faith is strong;" "may God bless our union;" symbol of interconnection and eternity
- Vines/honeysuckle: love that keeps growing
- Twisted stem: two become one
- Flowers: "may I court you?" token of affection
- Wheel: representing the ship's wheel or cartwheel, professes the ability to make a good living
- Anchor: "my heart is steadfast"
- Dragon: protection
- One heart: "I profess my love for you"
- Double hearts: reciprocated love
- Heart-shaped bowl: promises a bountiful life
- Bell: "will you marry me?"
- Chain: together forever; sign of fidelity
- Links on a chain: in how many years we will marry/how many children we will have
- Keyhole: "here is the key to my heart and home;" sign of security
- Lock: locked in my heart; "I will protect you"

FORGET
ME
NOT

THE ENDLESS KNOT OF

LOVE

Breast, this Sacred LOVE doth so Real as the joys Beginning, NEVER, lewels none can

VIRTUE that we prove. None are Endures for SEVER PLACE thereof Embrace.

LOVE is a VIRTUE the many pleasures ENDING. EVER. Shall alter DEATH the fruits

amongst of LOVE for this Matchless is love & worth Commanding. Still

A link

96

The Lover's Knot

Originally a favor tied from ribbons (at one time ripped from the bride's dress), the lover's knot spread among wedding guests the luck that attracts to newlyweds and was worn proudly on a lapel, warping eventually into the boutonnière. Knots are for binding together, and the traditional lover's knot is impressively complex, comprising two knots, with two bows on each side and two ends. Natural knots entwined in willow are considered a powerful love charm by gypsies that, tied by fairy folk, should not be untied by humankind.

By hiding the knot in a girl's bed, a man hoped to win her love. In wedding rituals, the knot as symbol of union is said to keep out malevolent forces and tie in good luck—not for nothing is marriage known as getting hitched or spliced.

In India 24 white cotton threads are woven together. During the ceremony, the resulting cord is looped around the right hands of bride and groom as the priest sprinkles holy water over the couple, literally tying the knot. The head piece of the bride's sari is tied to the end of the groom's shawl before they take seven steps around the holy fire. In Italy, an ornately tied bow decorates the entrance of the church, hinting at the spiritual ties that will bind the couple. During the wedding feast that follows, guests snack on *wanda*, delicious twists, or knots, of dough deep fried and sprinkled with sugar.

Tiny sweet knot pastries, *Schlatemer Rickli*, also make an appearance at Swiss wedding parties, served again next day when the women of both families gather to gossip over coffee.

Defiant Elopement

The Chinese-inspired willow pattern that adorned so many cobalt blue and white plates from around 1780 tells the story of defiant lovers determined to marry. Many variations of the design exist, but on all you can spot the fleeing couple, love birds in the sky, a willow tree, and the boat in which the secretly betrothed paramors make their escape.

The Story of the Willow Pattern

In ancient China, there once was a beautiful maiden named Koong-see. She fell in love with her father's secretary, a young man known as Chang. When her father found out about the love match, he forbade the marriage, and commanded his daughter to wed a wealthy suitor of his choice. She refused to comply with his wishes, and so the father imprisoned his daughter in a little house within an apple orchard. From here she sent a message to her lover, "Gather thy blossom ere it be stolen," and he crept into the orchard and freed her.

They are seen fleeing across a bridge during the season in which the willow tree sheds its leaves, carrying her dowry, a box of jewels. The angry father, accompanied by a band of soldiers, is in pursuit. The lovers escape on the ship to an island, but after they are discovered and the groom slaughtered, the distraught bride-to-be envelops herself in flames and perishes. At her death two doves appear in the sky, symbols of the souls of the lovers united at last in a Chinese sign of married love everlasting.

Right: 18th-century Mughal manuscript, depicting a couple's elopement

> "*Rather would I have the love songs of romantic ages...rather an elopement by ladder and rope on a moonlight night, followed by the father's curse, mother's moans...than correctness and propriety measured by yardsticks.*"
>
> Emma Goldman

Shedding a Tear

"It used to be in the programme of weddings that brides should weep in the vestry at least when signing their maiden name for the last time, and perhaps at the breakfast as well. But we have changed all that. Tears are now bad form."

Mrs. Humphry, early twentieth-century etiquette queen

It's not just the mother of the bride who is expected to shed a few tears on the big day. Brides' tears are considered lucky, presaging rains that water crops and stimulate new growth. In many countries, brides carry a (mostly) ceremonial handkerchief beautifully worked with inset lace and embroidery to complement her outfit as well as dab the eyes, mop the best man's brow, or make young attendants presentable.

Sentimental brides will have one made, as in days gone by, from a memorable family gown, passed on and embroidered each time with the bride's name and marriage date. In Belgium it is displayed ceremonially in a frame. Many brides present a handkerchief keepsake to mothers and bridal attendants as a memento of the occasion, embroidered with lucky emblems or words of thanks. Antique lace handkerchiefs are extra special—because each is unique, you can select them to suit the individual, perhaps monogrammed with initials, embroidered with a favorite flower or one from the bridal bouquet, a cross, or for the origins of its lace in Brussels, Lyon, or Devon. In Switzerland, the youngest bridesmaids are furnished with colored handkerchiefs that guests "buy" to add funds to the nuptial pot.

Bride Quilts

"Good linen is a real joy."

from *The Home Book*, 1950

In the past, quilts were most often stitched to fill a young woman's hope chest. Sometimes the girl herself worked on them, learning as she went traditional patterns and techniques. More often a grandmother, maiden aunt, or mother would donate a quilt, it being considered bad fortune in some regions of North America for a prospective bride to work her own covers. From the 1840s and 50s onward, bride quilts were often "album" pieces with squares donated by different women, each a remembrance of a place or event personal to them and the bride-to-be.

Some album quilts were the result of sociable quilting bees, or "frolics," in which girls would stitch "friendship" quilts for their peers or eligible young men. Such communal quilting parties brought with them license for flirtation: young men would escort girls home after the session. A bride hoped to make or receive thirteen quilts: twelve everyday comforters to cover the new home's beds (in winter a family would use up to eight quilts on a single bed), plus one extra special quilt, perhaps elaborately appliquéd, reserved for the marital bed. On the marital bed might also turn up a wedding shawl: frontier women, ever mindful of the need to be practical, were wont to wear everyday dresses for their wedding, trimming the outfit with a colorful paisley shawl that doubled as a bed cover.

Traditional Bride Quilt Motifs

Certain motifs and quilting patterns were deemed particularly suitable, even auspicious, for a wedding quilt. When one of these quilts was finished, tradition had it that unmarried girls or young men (or two of each) would each take a corner, and a cat be thrown into the center. The person closest to where puss jumped out would marry within the year.

Auspicious designs

- Heart: including these before the engagement was announced was considered unlucky
- Dove: representative of peace; purity
- Pineapple: stands for life and fertility; a sign of hospitality
- Cornucopia: to bring about abundance
- Honeysuckle: entwined love and devotion
- Rose: true love
- Tulip: adoration
- Meadow lily: love
- Pine tree: stability and rootedness
- Circles and the Double Wedding Ring design: love without beginning and end; a journey
- Names and date: sometimes stitched in the bride's own hair

Motifs to avoid

- Turkey Tracks or Wandering Foot designs: risks marring a marriage with wanderlust and instability

Pennsylvania Wreath quilt

EXTRACT FROM

The Quilters

by

PATRICIA COOPER &
NORMA BRADLEY ALLEN

When a girl was thinkin' on
marryin,' and we all done a lot of
that, she had to start thinkin' on
getting her quilts pieced. The way
I done mine was real nice, I think.
Papa had laid up a beautiful arbor
with the brush he had cleared from
the land. It was set up a ways back
of the house. Well, I jest went out
under that arbor, set up my frame,
and went to quiltin' outdoors…

Anyways, what I was doin' was
settin' there under that quiltin'
arbor one spring afternoon, April

fourteenth, just quiltin' and
dreamin' a dream on ever stitch
and just plannin' who might share
'em with me.

And this deep, fine voice says,
"Pardon me, ma'am, but I've been
seein' you out here ever day for
weeks and I jest got up my nerve
to come over and speak to you and
see what you were workin' on with
such care."

Lordy girl, I married him and,
as I recall it now, that was the
longest speech he ever said at one
time to this day.

The Bachelorette Party

Today many brides don't marry until their thirties, so there's more disposable income for elaborate get-togethers with girlfriends. But the best send-off parties can just be a night in with a DVD and your best friends.

Mendhi ritual: Hire a henna artist to decorate hands and feet with swirly, lacy filigree work. Then sit still, sip, and chat as you wait for the paste to dry: the longer you keep from moving, the darker the color, and the darker the color the more loving the husband! Make sure the bride's hands and feet are the most beautifully adorned.

Creative crockery: Hold a party at a plate-painting studio, decorating a set of special plates with dates and hearts to mark the occasion.

Fortune-telling: Have a palmist and tarot reader join you for an evening of love divination and discovery.

Spa day: Lie back and be pampered. Many spas run bride-to-be packages for you and a friend (or your Mom) or sampler sessions for small groups, complete with Champagne.

Pampering pedicures: Book a beauty appointment for manicures and pedicures *chez vous*.

Go horseback riding: Be ten years old again, spending a day in the saddle. Follow with a pampering night in to ease saddle sores. ☞

☞ *Pajama party:* Bring teddy and pajamas, tell ghost stories, have pillow fights and a midnight feast, and stay up 'til dawn and finish with some of the following movies for a bachelorette night in:

- High Society
- My Big Fat Greek Wedding
- My Best Friend's Wedding
- Philadelphia Story
- How to Marry A Millionaire
- Seven Brides for Seven Brothers
- Father of the Bride
- Monsoon Wedding
- La Belle et La Bête
- While You Were Sleeping
- Bride and Prejudice
- Sense and Sensibility
- From Here to Eternity
- Sleepless in Seattle
- Four Weddings and a Funeral

Bridal Showers

The bridal shower may have been originally a Dutch tradition. If a father did not approve his daughter's match and refused a dowry, friends might get together to shower the bride with all she would need for her future life. Now friends assist the bride by bringing small gifts and advice to furnish each area of her married life: favorite recipes and ingredients for the kitchen, utensils for the garden, lingerie for the bedroom.

Informal parties complement the theme with guessing and forfeit games lubricated by wine, sweet and savory treats and, of course, cake (bake bridal shower charms into the batter to determine who will marry next). Family recipes have always formed part of a bride's dowry. The honey-spice cakes baked by Polish women early in December, *piernik*, were closely guarded family secrets that formed an essential part of the dowry even after families settled in the United States.

Shower Themes

- 1950s housewife: aprons and headscarves obligatory

- Bedroom siren: bring massage oils, lingerie, and love poetry

- Breakfast club: a morning party for gifts of waffle irons, coffee, napkins, and smoothie ingredients

- Picnic: stock a hamper

- Poetry slam: contribute a poem about the bride

- Spice of life: gifts to keep a marriage hot, from chiles to love manuals

- Life's a beach: flip flops, sun cream, and shades for beach bums

- Games cupboard: supply the essentials—playing cards, checkers, chess

- Stock a library: donate your favorite read or tunes

- Photo album: provide memorable images of the couple

- Cookie cutting: come with dough and a recipe

- Hardware share: for nuts and bolts, hammers and tools

- Christmas is coming: bring something shiny

Champagne Cocktail

This glorious drink is ideal for giggling girlfriends at a shower or bachelorette party. If your wedding is a select cocktail affair, this classic is one of the best options.

Makes one glass

1 tsp sugar
2 dashes Angostura Bitters
1 shot cognac
Champagne
slice of orange

1 Place the sugar cube in a Champagne flute and drop the bitters on top.

2 Pour over the cognac, then fill with Champagne. Garnish with the slice of orange.

Pitchers of Iced Tea

A genteel 1920s-style beverage for guests avoiding alcohol and ideal as an accompaniment to cake.

Makes 1 pitcher

2 bags Assam or strong, high quality tea
large carton pure apple juice, chilled
2 lemons
1 apple

1 orange
¼ cucumber
handful fresh mint leaves
ice
sugar to taste

1 Place the teabags in a large teapot or pitcher, and pour over just-boiled water. Cover and leave to brew for about 5 minutes.

2 Pour the tea into a large pitcher, discarding the teabags. Leave to cool.

3 Add an equal amount of chilled apple juice and the juice of one lemon.

4 Wash the fruit, then quarter and core the apple. Slice all the fruit and cucumber; add to the pitcher with the mint sprigs. Chill and serve with ice cubes and sugar, if desired.

Royal wedding breakfast menu for marriage of Princess Maud of Norway (daughter of Edward VII) to Prince Carl of Denmark (later King Haakon VII of Norway) on July 22, 1896

THE
ROYAL WEDDING BREAKFAST

WEDNESDAY, 22ND JULY, 1896

POTAGES.
A la Princesse.
Vermicelle à la Windsor.

ENTRÉES (CHAUDES).
Côtelettes d'agneau à l'Italienne.
Aiguilettes de Canetons aux pois.

RELEVÉS.
Filets de Bœuf à la Napolitaine.
Poulets gras aux Cressons.

ENTRÉES (FROIDES).
Chaudfroids de Volaille sur Croûtes.
Salades d'Homard.
Jambons decoupés à l'Aspic.
Langues decoupées à l'Aspic.
Mayonaises de Volaille.
Roulades de Veau à la Gelée.

———

Haricots Verts. Epinards.

———

Gelées et Crêmes.
Patisserie assorties.

The Wedding Brunch

Bringing together favorite people to share delicious food and raise glasses in a toast to a long and happy life is the one must-do for wedding celebrations around the globe. The traditional wedding "breakfast" is so named because nineteenth-century weddings took place early in the day.

In the U.S., this tradition has evolved into the wedding brunch the day after the ceremony or a rehearsal dinner. The latter takes place before the ceremony, and is given by the bride and groom for the bridal party to celebrate their participation in the festivities. Try one of these alternatives to a sit-down meal.

Wine and cheese party: Good wine merely requires rustic loaves, local and continental cheeses, and stacks of grapes

Spit-roasted hog: Find a specialty caterer for a meal that's an event in itself

Farmhouse supper: Hold a harvest home with cold meats, quiches, chutneys, and a Victorian trifle or summer pudding

Smorgasbord or Russian zakuski table: Major on Beluga and eggplant caviar, smoked salmon and blinis accompanied by several varieties of flavored vodka

Sushi: Try this as delicious finger food for stand-up buffets

Cornish cream tea: Fill to sating on scones, strawberry jam, and clotted cream. Equally good with tea or Champagne

Left: *Artists' Party*, by P. S. Krøyer

Outdoor Decor

Set the scene for more informal outdoor receptions by flagging up the entrance to the space with quirky decorative touches that shout "party-time."

Marking out the party space
* Plant seaside windmills in large terracotta pots
* Sew homemade decorations themed to match the wedding, in toile de Jouy, classic stripes, gingham, checks, or chintzy florals
* Inflate huge bunches of helium balloons (and weight down well)
* Fly a flotilla of kites to signal the party venue from far off
* Hang bamboo and metal wind chimes from tree branches
* Plant bamboo canes in the ground and attach long multicolored streamers to blow in the breeze

Outdoor lighting
* Create a walk of flaming torches
* Drape trees and marquees with outdoor flower lights and light ropes
* Suspend nightlights in glass jars from canes
* Light glass storm lamps
* Set up a bubble machine and light it from behind
* Round off the evening with a bonfire and fireworks display, handing out sparklers

Eating outdoors
* Weight outdoor tablecloths with arrangements of beach pebbles
* Set out bales of straw for informal rustic seating
* Set up easel-style blackboards with menu options chalked up to save on individual cartes
* Choose picnic tables with holes in the middle, and put up wide ornamental Oriental parasols

Tell me whom you love and
I'll tell you who you are.

African-American proverb

A Canopy

In the Judaic wedding tradition, bride and groom stand beneath a cotton wedding canopy, or *chuppah*, often embroidered and adorned with flowers. Indeed, a wedding can take place anywhere, as long as bride and groom, their parents and, the rabbi, are gathered beneath this sacred bower.

This cloistered place is envisaged as being as conducive to inner peace as a walled garden—maybe even the garden of Eden—and as protective and nurturing as a womb, from which the newborn couple emerges. Marriage, too, can be seen as a protective canopy, a safe space of shared beliefs and faith in which to explore each other and forge new relationships—with in-laws, with children, and with yourself. French wedding couples, too, wait in church beneath a canopy of silk, and in traditional Hindu weddings across India, bride and groom sit beneath a richly embroidered cotton canopy, or *mandaps*, embellished with mandala-like geometrical devices and floral motifs, or within a real canopy of foliage woven from bamboo, mango, and banana leaves, all plants that connote fruitful abundance.

Even in the middle of the city, Spanish couples often flee the wedding festivities to an arbor of flowers on a terrace or rooftop for a little seclusion after a whirlwind day and before making their final escape from the wedding feast.

Right: *Wedding at St-Roch in Paris*, by Eugene Lami and Charles Heath

Outdoor Celebrations

A summer wedding doesn't have to be a formal affair. Free it up a bit and see what fun there is to be had when guests are more relaxed. *Que la fête commence!*

Picnic party
Supply each guest's party with a gingham tablecloth and wicker hamper loaded with buffet treats: tarts and salads, good bread and cheese, and chilled Champagne.

Bring-your-own barbecue
Supply the marinated meat, fish, and veggie kebabs, then have guests contribute salads and side dishes for a less costly celebration.

Farm camping
Find a friendly farmer willing to lend a field and have friends and family pitch tents for a relaxed festival vibe with a freedom that kids adore.

Crayfish party
Hold a Swedish-style evening crayfish party, hanging paper lanterns under dusky skies and laying tables with salads and fish dishes, pies filled with summer berries and topped with vanilla cream, and crayfish, of course!

Clam bake
Stake out a space on the beach with balloons on sticks and brightly-colored garlands or flame torches then settle in for an evening of campfires and seafood.

My Mother's House

by

COLETTE

Where did I get my violent passion for rustic wedding breakfasts? What ancestor bequeathed to me, via my frugal parents, a positively religious fervor for stewed rabbit, leg of mutton with garlic, soft-boiled eggs in red wine, all served between barn walls draped with buff sheets decorated with branches of red June roses? I am only thirteen, and the familiar menu of these four o'clock repasts does not appall me. Glass basins filled with loaf sugar are strewn about the table: everyone knows that they are so placed in order that the guests, between courses, may suck lumps of sugar soaked in wine, an infallible method of loosening the tongue and of renewing the appetite. Bouilloux and Labbé, gargantuan freaks, indulge in a guzzling match here as at all weddings. Labbé drinks white wine from a pail used for milking the cows, and Bouilloux is offered an entire leg of mutton, which he consumes unaided, leaving nothing but the bare bone.

What with songs, feasting, and carousing, Adrienne's wedding is a lovely wedding. Five meat courses, three sweets, and the tiered wedding cake surmounted by a trembling plaster rose. Since four o'clock the open doorway of the barn has framed the green pond shaded by elms, and a patch of sky now gradually flushing with the evening glow. Adrienne Septmance, dark, and unfamiliar in her cloud of tulle, leans langorously against her husband's shoulder and wipes the sweat from a shining face. A tall, bony peasant bellows patriotic songs, "Paris must be saved! Paris must be saved!" and he encounters looks of awe because his voice is powerful, and sad, and he himself comes from so great a distance: "Just think! A man from Dampierre-sous-Bouhy! At least thirty miles from here!" The swallows dart and scream above the drinking cattle. The bride's mother is weeping for no particular reason. Julie David has stained her dress; the dresses of the four Follet girls are as blue as phosphorus in the gathering gloom. The candles will not be lighted until the ball begins. A happiness in advance of any years, a subtle happiness of satiated greed, keeps me sitting there peacefully gorged with rabbit stew, boiled chicken, and sweetened wine.

"If you are going to a wedding, you don't need to eat three days before and three days after."

Russian saying

Dressing a Party Tent

If your budget won't stretch to an embroidered Egyptian pavilion or a mirrored Rajasthani marquee, transform a standard canopy or pole tent with inventive decorative touches.

Lighting

- String up fairy or flower lights
- Hire a disco ball
- Scour thrift shops for kitsch chandeliers
- Illuminate Moroccan pierced-metal lanterns
- Project slides of romantic scenes (gushing waterfalls, tropical beaches at sunset, city skylines, etc.) or the couple as children

From the ceiling

- Pin up sparkly saris to form a false ceiling
- Suspend embroidered canopies
- Peg single gerberas onto cord, criss-crossing from one corner of the roof to the other
- Tightly wind tent poles with ivy and evergreens
- Fix up jingling bead curtains to cordon off areas

On the floor

- Lay Indian *dhurries* and Persian carpets
- Strew lavender heads to scent the air when trampled
- Create a carpet of rosemary or bay leaves, as strewn along a couple's path away from church

To scent the air

- Place up to eight drops of essential oil in the water bowl of a vaporizer and light the candle beneath, or use an electric diffuser
- Scented candles are a must

Decorative seating

- Tie mop-headed hydrangeas or bunches of lavender to the back of each chair with satin ribbon
- Group beanbags and cushions to create a sociable lounging zone

Wedding Favors

A bridal couple is lucky. If, in the old days, people used to try to steal a sprig from the bouquet or a touch of the bride as she emerged down the aisle for luck, now bride and groom distribute party favors to apportion their good fortune more equitably. The classic party favor is a *bonbonnière*, pastel-colored sugared almonds tied up in a frou frou of pastel netting. This Italian custom celebrates the bitter (almonds) sweet (sugar coating) union that is marriage (sugar almonds are also showered over newlyweds). The parcels contain an auspicious odd number of almonds: three stands for the couple with their firstborn; five, the ingredients for a successful marriage—love, fidelity, fertility, happiness, and longevity. Here are more frivolous ideas for lucky amulets to keep you in your guest's thoughts.

For fun on the day

- Pots of bubbles to blow
- Disposable cameras

To take home

- Heart-shaped bathbombs that explode with petals
- Packets of seeds matching flowers in the bouquet
- Aphrodisiac bath oils to spread the passion

- Mini heart soaps
- Heart-shaped lavender bags; fill with spicy cinnamon and cloves for winter weddings
- Miniature Welsh love spoons

Edible treats

- Chocolate truffles in packaging bearing the couple's image
- Gingerbread bride and groom, with white icing and silver ball decorations
- Personalized cupcakes piped with initials
- Heart-shaped sugar cubes
- Miniature bottles of cognac labeled with the date of the wedding
- Pots of locally produced honey with specially designed labels

For kids at heart

- "Loveheart" candies
- Hershey's kisses
- Italian *baci* chocolate pastilles; each comes wrapped in its own love note
- Heart-shaped jelly beans
- Red gummy-shaped lips

Classic Cocktails

Not all wedding traditions consider Champagne the drink of
choice. In Holland guests sip on a spiced wine punch known
as "bride's tears." Instead of serving Champagne, why not
host a cocktail party, offering only the most
classy classics? The couple who cares hire a
"mixologist" to ensure
perfection every time.

Cosmopolitan

Combine 1¼ measures each vodka and cranberry juice with 1 measure Cointreau (or Triple Sec) and the juice of 1 lime. Garnish with a twist of orange or a few cranberries.

Dry Martini

Add 3 measures gin to ½ measure dry vermouth. Garnish with an olive.

Manhattan

Mix 2 measures Vermouth Rosso with 1 measure whisky. Add a dash of Angostura bitters. Garnish with a maraschino cherry.

Margarita

Shake 2 measures each tequila and lime juice with 1 measure Triple Sec and ice. Strain into a salt-dipped glass and garnish with a wedge of lime.

Long Island Ice Tea

To ice add a good squeeze of lime juice, then ¼ measure Triple Sec, ¾ measure each of gin, white rum, vodka, tequila, and fresh orange juice. Top up with Coke.

Domestic Goddesses

"Hail bride and bridegroom, children both of Jove,
With fruitful joys let Hera bless your love.
Let Venus furnish you with full desires,
Add vigour to your wills and fuel your fires."

from "Wedding Song" by Theocritus

Hera: Ancient Greek goddess of marriage, Hera is the personal protective spirit that guards every woman, especially during childbirth. On her wedding day to Zeus, greatest of the Greek gods, she was presented with a tree of golden apples by Gaia, goddess of the earth and fertility, and her wedding night lasted three hundred years! Hera is best known for her anger at husband Zeus' amorous adventures, of which there were many, and her numerous schemes to humiliate him.

Juno: Roman equivalent of Hera, Juno is wife of Jupiter and goddess of marriage. She governed childbirth and light, and is the figure in the pantheon women petitioned for protection. The favorite month to marry for modern brides is still Juno's month, June, thought to augur prosperity and happiness (recent research shows women are more likely to conceive in early summer).

Lakshmi: The Hindu goddess of good fortune, fertility, prosperity, beauty, and success is dear to Hindu brides for, in each of her incarnations, she is the faithful wife of Vishnu, among other couplings as Dharani to his Parashurama, Radha, then Rukmini to his Krishna, and Sita for his Rama. These two are the emblematic married couple, each defining the other, with Vishnu a sun-god and Lakshmi rising out of the ocean water; she is often depicted with her water-rooted flower, the lotus, since another incarnation saw her as Padma, a lotus.

St. Bridget: Although brides in England would visit fertility wells dedicated to St. Bridget after their marriage, this fifth-century patron saint of Ireland is not the patron saint of brides. But the mythology surrounding her has been intertwined and conflated with another Brigid, the mythical Brid, Brigit, Bridgit, Birgit, or Brigantia, goddess of the sun, fire, and the hearth, of light, abundance, and prosperity, and mother of the Celtic gods. St. Bridget's feast day is February 1, which corresponds with the festival of light at the start of the Celtic season of Imbolc, harbinger of the returning light and of spring, and the traditional time for courting that sees fruition in an early summer marriage. The Christianized Bridget is also regarded as a contemporary of the Blessed Virgin, who as midwife and wet nurse to the infant Jesus is called upon by women in childbirth like Hera/Juno. In abbreviated form, St. Bridget has churches named for her as St. Bride, which only adds to the confusion. The most famed is Sir Christopher Wren's church of St. Bride in Fleet Street, London, which has a spire shaped like the tiers of a wedding cake.

If Music Be the Food of Love...

...play on, wrote the Bard in *Twelfth Night*, his wedding romp. For how can you celebrate love and lust without music? Here are some inventive options for live bands and DJ selections to reflect every taste, age group, and heritage.

Great live music options

- Cajun band
- Steel pan band
- Swing orchestra with vocalist
- Harp player
- String quintet
- Sinatra-style crooner
- Irish folk ensemble
- Opera singer for tear-jerking arias
- Klezmer band
- Jump jive band, plus lindyhop dance instructor
- Albanian brass wedding band; follow them in a procession
- Mariachi musicians to serenade the tables
- Scottish piper
- Salsa band with dance tutors
- Jazz quartet
- Andean panpipers
- Hoedown with caller
- Fairground barrel organ
- Ceilidh band

Top tunes for wedding DJs

- "Love Train" The O'Jays
- "I Do, I Do, I Do, I Do, I Do?" Abba
- "Move Closer" Phyllis Nelson
- "Rock Your Baby" George McCrae
- "How 'Bout Us" Champaign
- "Best of My Love" The Emotions
- "Just the Two of Us" Bill Withers
- "Love Cats" The Cure

BRIDAL SONG

Words by Mark Lemon.

He Will Praise His Lady

GUIDO GUINIZELLI
TRANSLATED BY DANTE GABRIEL ROSSETTI

Yea, let me praise my lady whom I love:
Likening her unto the lily and rose:
Brighter than morning star her visage glows;
She is beneath even as her Saint above.

She is as the air in summer which God wove
Of purple and of vermilion glorious;
As gold and jewels richer than man knows.
Love's self, being love for her, must holier prove.
Ever as she walks she hath a sober grace,

Making bold men abashed and good men glad;
If she delight thee not, thy heart must err.
No man dare look on her, his thoughts being base:
Nay, let me say even more than I have said;—
No man could think base thoughts who looked on her.

Dressing Tiny Bridesmaids

The bride's attendants are no longer compelled to dress all the same. Once, bridesmaids had to be tricked out all in white as a decoy against bad spirits with an eye on the bride. So don't confine the youngest ones to restrictive starched matching dresses; throw caution to the wind and dress them as extras from *A Midsummer Night's Dream*.

Fairy princesses: Accessorize billowing net fairy dresses with diamante crowns and fabric or feather wings. Winter fairies in shades of russet, plum, and crimson can look even more special than their regular pastel-shaded cousins.

Ballerinas: Send off to ballet suppliers for tulle tutus and seamed ballet tights, slippers that lace up the leg (perhaps adorned with extra ribbon rosebuds or sequins), and cashmere wrapover cardigans for chilly days.

Putti: Cherubic enough as they are, tiny attendants have only to put on a white dress and halo of feathers to guarantee gasps of delight when they walk down the aisle. This look works well for little boys—think white suits and canvas pumps.

Flower fairies: Take inspiration from the illustrations in Cicely Mary Barker's *Flower Fairy* books from the early part of the twentieth century, basing outfits on flower fairies or elves that match the blooms in your bouquet. Complete each outfit with a fresh-flower circlet and simple posy that looks handpicked from the garden.

Making a Bridesmaid's Flower Ball

A pretty flower ball looks delightful carried by young bridesmaids—select flowers to match the color and style of the dresses. Hang them to decorate the reception room, or on the ends of pews in a church. (Caution: because of the pins, do not give to children under three.) If you prefer real flowers, wire each bloom before pinning onto the ball.

MATERIALS
- *Selection of silk flowers*
- *4-in/10-cm diameter polystyrene ball*
- *Small glass beads*
- *20in/50cm matching gauze ribbon*

TOOLS
- *Craft scissors*
- *Dressmaker's pins*
- *Tape measure*
- *Sewing kit*

1 Carefully separate each silk flower from its stalk, snipping off with scissors if necessary.

2 Thread a small bead onto a pin, then spear the center of the largest flower, and press onto the polystyrene ball. Repeat with all the large flowers, spacing them evenly.

3 To make multicolored flowers, layer three or four different colored heads together on a pin, the largest at the bottom, before pinning onto the ball.

4 Continue pinning single and layered flowers to the ball, being sure to spread the colors evenly across its surface.

5 Add individual green leaves to fill in any spaces.

6 To make the handle, cut a 30cm/12in length of ribbon and fold into a loop. Stitch together the ends with a row of running stitch, then draw up the thread. Stitch the gathered end to secure, and fasten it to the ball, using several pins to make it secure.

7 Cut the ends of the remaining ribbon into fish tails. Fold the ribbon in half and gather the fold with running stitch as before. Pin the gathered end to the polystyrene ball directly opposite the handle at the bottom of the ball.

Summer Floral Displays

- Mass roadside weeds and hedgerow foliage in shiny tin cans with labels soaked off (be careful not to pick wildflowers).
- Float rose petals and flower candles in low, wide glass bowls.
- Pile blowsy peonies into colored vases.
- Line up rows of pressed-glass pitchers and tumblers each containing different ferns.
- Pin up sprigs or branches from lemon trees Sardinian style (or use tiny trees in pots).
- Bend wire into heart shapes and thread with rose petals or dried rose buds, then suspend from the top with pink or green ribbon.
- Anchor every style queen's favorite—orchids—in pebbles.
- Source tall glass vases in jewel colors and let them steal the show by filling with stems of foliage.
- Fill children's tin beach buckets with pebbles and tall thin candles.
- Plant a fishtank with white lacecap hydrangeas; they resemble frilly white clouds.
- Fill a container with herbs and classic country garden blooms.
- Hang a flower garland for every guest, Indian style, over the back of each chair.
- Transplant elegant topiary balls or box into mini stone urns.
- Fill tall pitchers with different varieties of sunflowers.
- Plant different combinations of herbs: mix various types of mint, sage with rosemary, or dill with cilantro.
- Forego the flowers for feathers: fill tall glass vases with white feathers for a frothy dream of a display.

Now you will feel no rain,
for each of you will be a shelter to the other.
Now you will feel no cold,
For each of you will be warmth to the other.
Now there is no loneliness for you;
Now there is no more loneliness.

Now you are two bodies,
but there is only one life before you.
Go now to your dwelling place,
to enter into your days together.
And may your days be good
and long on the earth.

Apache marriage song

Marriage of Pocahontas and John Rolfe by E. Boyd Smith

Summer Flowers for Bouquets

Roses: The archetypal symbol of love and a flower sacred to the goddess Venus. Try to find scented varieties and contrast tiny spray roses with opulent, open tea roses. The soothing scent lifts the spirits, beats stress, and brings out femininity.

Gardenias: Classically romantic in color and shape, all underpinned with an exotic scent.

Peonies: Romantically heavy with petals. When fully open they droop langorously, and are just as effective when in bud. Colors range from shell pink to deep crimson. Ancient Greeks thought them divine in origin.

Cornflowers: Deep blue flowers with country associations that suit a cottage-like bouquet.

Delphiniums: Tall spires of flowers with a delicate, old-fashioned ambience.

Love-in-a-Mist: Frothy filigree foliage with turquoise or white flowers for a hazy mistlike effect.

Honeysuckle: A heavenly scent to twine into a bouquet that lasts for an entire day. The flower remedy honeysuckle is said to focus the mind in the present and help you cherish memories. The traditional French symbol of intertwining love and marriage.

Lavender: Look for ornate butterfly blooms, or choose white varieties that seem particularly appropriate for brides. The scent can help calm nervous tension.

Sweet Peas: Nothing could look, well, sweeter, in summer than a wealth of sugar-almond-hued sweet peas tied with a satin ribbon. Ensure the varieties you choose are scented.

Lady in Red

In parts of India, and in China and Korea, brides dress in red, the color of prosperity, good luck, and joy, and across the Middle East, *mendhi*, henna, is etched onto hands and feet in rich mahogany patterns, the deeper the red, the more loving the husband, so the saying goes. Scarlet women in the West might shun tradition and choose to marry in red to make a statement of independence still guaranteed to raise an eyebrow among wedding guests.

Some American brides were said to favor red dresses during the Revolutionary War, as a mark of defiance to symbolize the independence that the Colonists desired. But why not wear red, the color of fiery passion and of that ultimate love token, the red rose?

A red thread is still considered to have protective powers in some parts of the United Kingdom, where it might be knotted onto babies' clothing to deflect the evil eye. It is said that if you find a strand of red ribbon or wool on your wedding morning, wish for luck in love on it and carry it with you all day. In China a bright red paper good-luck banner inscribed with the character "Double happiness" is displayed prominently where the couple can't avoid seeing it. Other traditional bold and beautiful technicolors for wedding gowns include yellow silk, a must have in south India, highlighted with rubies and emeralds. Green is still a no-no, however, carrying inferences that one might have been rolling a little too enthusiastically on the grass.

Dorani

Once, long ago in India, there lived a perfume seller with a
beautiful daughter, Dorani. She, and her friend, a fairy, sang
and danced so beautifully that Indra, king of fairyland, was
enchanted. Dorani's hair was as spun gold scented with roses.
Being so long, lustrous, and heavy, the hair caused her
discomfort, so she cut off a lock and cast it into the river,
wrapped in a leaf. It so happened that the king's son,
drinking on the riverbank while hunting, smelt the exquisite
odor and retrieved the perfumed parcel from the water.

That night, the prince seemed distracted. His father
questioned him. From his breast the prince plucked the lock
of hair and held it high; it dazzled as the light shone through
it. "Unless I win and marry the maid who owns this lock of
hair, I must die," he declared.

Next day, the king sent heralds throughout the land to find
the girl with hair like spun gold. At last Dorani heard the
news. She told her father, "As the hair is mine, I must marry
the prince—the king decrees it—but you must tell him that
though I will remain at the palace each day after the
wedding, I must spend every night here at home."

The old man agreed, knowing she was wiser than him, and
when summoned to the palace, broke the news to the king.

Amused, the king agreed, and the wedding was celebrated with great rejoicing.

The prince was overjoyed at first to spend all day every day with his bride. But soon he became dismayed; she would do nothing but sit on a stool, head bowed to her knees. He could not persuade Dorani to say a word. Every evening she returned to her father's house, and each morning came back to the palace soon after dawn. All the time she never said a word, nor as much as looked at her husband. One evening, the troubled prince confessed his sorrows to an old gardener, "I have married a wife as lovely as the stars, but she will neither speak to nor look at me. I know not what to do."

The old man wandered off, then returned with five or six small packets. He gave them to the prince, saying, "Tomorrow, when your bride leaves the palace, sprinkle powder from one of these packets over yourself and you will become invisible. Follow her."

The prince tucked the packets into his turban and thanked the old man. When Dorani left the following evening, the prince took out one packet of powder and sprinkled it over himself. Invisible, he followed her home to the scent-seller's residence. He followed her inside, and to her room, where she washed at two basins, one of water, one of attar of roses. She ate a bowl of curds, then dressed in a robe of silver, wound strings of pearls around herself, then crowned her hair with a wreath of roses. She sat upon a stool over which there stood a canopy of silk, which she drew about her, calling, "Fly, stool, to the palace of Indra." ☞

As the stool rose into the air, the prince seized a leg. They soon arrived at the home of the fairy, Dorani's friend, as beautifully dressed as his bride. She cried in astonishment, when she saw the stool flying crooked, "Why, the stool will not fly straight; you have been talking to your husband."

When Dorani declared that she had not said a word, the fairy sat beside her, and immediately they flew to Indra's palace. All night the women sang and danced before Indra, as a magic lute played the most enchanting music. The prince was entranced. Just before dawn the fairy king gave the signal to stop. Girl and fairy climbed onto the stool, and flew back to the scent-seller's shop. The prince hurried away, arriving at the palace just before Dorani, who simply sat down as before, head bowed, silent as ever.

"I had a curious dream last night," started the prince, and described all he'd seen. Dorani kept silent, only looking up when he described her beautiful singing. That evening, the prince again made himself invisible and followed Dorani. Next morning again he described to her his "dream." When he had finished, Dorani gazed at him, saying, "Did you dream this, or were you there?"

"I was there," he replied.

"But why do you follow me?"

"Because I love you and to be with you is happiness."

Dorani's eyelids quivered, but she said no more until just before leaving that night, "If you love me, prove it by not following me tonight."

The prince did as she wished. That evening the stool flew so unsteadily that the fairy declared, "There is only one reason for this—you have been talking to your husband."

"Yes," Dorani replied, "Oh yes, I have spoken." And said no more.

That night Dorani sang so gloriously that Indra rose up and offered the girl her heart's desire. After a silence, Dorani spoke, "Give me the magic lute."

Indra was displeased—it was his most valued possession—but true to his word, he handed it over, saying, "Never come here again; having taken so great a thing, how will you be content with lesser gifts?"

Dorani bowed, took the lute, and flew back to the scent shop. When she arrived at the palace next morning, she asked the prince about his dreams. He laughed, overjoyed because she had spoken to him from her own free will. "I did not dream last night," he said, "But I am dreaming now; not of the past, but of how the future may be."

Dorani sat quietly all day, but answered when the prince spoke to her. That night, when it was time for her to leave, she remained seated. The prince drew close, speaking softly, "Are you not going home, Dorani?"

She rose and threw herself into his arms, whispering, "Never again will I leave you."

The prince won his bride, and though they never dealt more with the magic of fairyland, they learnt daily of the magic of love.

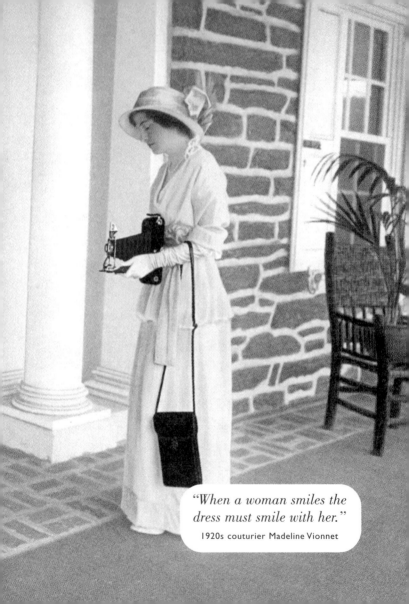

"When a woman smiles the dress must smile with her."

1920s couturier Madeline Vionnet

The Dress

"With time and patience the mulberry leaf becomes a silk gown."
Chinese proverb

Whether your preference is for a crisp white suit for cocktail-hour glam or a fairytale frou frou frock, this dream gown simply has to make you feel the best you've ever felt. It should leave your heart beating faster (your groom's too!) Surveys show that fewer brides are opting for the traditional floor-length "meringue." The modern miss selects a swooningly beautiful dress in a style that flatters, spends a little more than she can afford, and wears it afterward for parties and other special events. This continues a centuries-long tradition: in the past an occasion gown would form such a large investment that it would have to be worn, altered, dyed perhaps, and worn again over many years. (Modern brides use a dyeing service—look at the ads in the backs of wedding magazines.) Nothing could be more different for brides in some villages in southeast Oaxaca, Mexico, where the finely woven and costly marriage *huipile*, tunic, is carefully stored away after the wedding day only to be worn again after death, for the burial.

Commission a custom gown

Scour fashion magazines, making a collection of tear-sheets that sum up the style you'd like—a sleeve from here, a neckline from there. Visit fabric stores for inspiration, feeling the weight, holding up lengths of satin and silk ☞

against your skin to check the color tone, collecting swatches. When you find a pattern emerging of styles you like, seek recommendations for designers and dressmakers from friends and bridal websites. Visit the makers, look at their samples, ask questions, try things on. Eventually you'll find someone you feel can empathize with your vision. Allow up to three months from first visit to finished gown.

Wear a designer gown

Visit designer warehouse and sale stores for one-off catwalk creations that were too ornate or expensive to put into production, and returned boutique window pieces that were too special to sell. With the saving in cost, you might find you come away with a dress for the ceremony, another for the party, and a third for going-away.

Make your own

Though considered unlucky in some cultures, making your own dress can be immensely satisfying. The intense focus on intricate detail almost becomes a meditation, allowing you time out from the hectic pace of arrangements to ponder with every pin, tuck, and stitch the big day and your future life. Try to rid your mind of all else as you sew, or use a mantra, such as "love," to fix your mind in the moment and wipe away worries. Keep the pins you use as love tokens: pins employed in creating or altering a wedding dress are considered lucky for single women in search of a husband. In 1565 Mary Queen of Scots allowed her subjects to pick pins from her wedding gown to bring good fortune.

Taking the Veil

Donning a veil is for many women the ultimate expression of devotion and commitment that removes you from the everyday world of fashion and transports you to a fairytale dimension in which you are linked with your mother and hers before her. When you try on the veil, you become every bride that's ever been—a tear-jerking moment for even the most urbane sophisticate. Representing modesty and purity protected, the veil offers a space of quiet sanctuary—it has been envisaged as an enclosed garden—that shields its wearer from prying eyes and the attention of jealous spirits.

Veils saw a return to favor in the nineteenth century although the tradition is a long one: Roman ladies wore a head-to-toe red veil for the marriage ceremony, Greek brides a yellow covering. In China, a thousand-year tradition of wearing a lacy silk head cover with attached veil in red withstood the revolution of 1949.

In the U.S. bridal veils were popularized by Nelly Custis in 1797, when she married Laurence Lewis, the nephew of her grandfather, President George Washington. In Britain, it was Queen Victoria with her all white wedding in 1840 who made the veil the fashion statement of the moment. Her lace was the very fine Honiton variety made in Beer, Devon, in England. Honiton lace is made up of realistic motifs of flower buds, sprigs, and leaves with curling tendrils sewn onto a mesh ground. The motifs depicted might have spelt out a hidden message. Many hours' skilled labor were needed for each motif (often worked by different lacemakers, these were invisibly joined by an expert assembler).

The expense of such a handcrafted veil necessitated that it would become a valuable part of a bride's wealth, a dowry piece that still holds its value today. At times in the past, veils and the headpieces that held them—vintage veils unlike their modern counterparts have no set fixing point—became very showy. As the wedding gown grew simpler in silhouette and decoration during the early decades of the twentieth century, at its most pared in the straight up-and-down chemise dresses of the 1920s, veils got ever more blousy. Billowing silk tulle, Brussels or Lyon lace fell back from headpieces that fitted snugly over the forehead and were adorned with wax flowers and velvet leaves, metallic ribbon and gilding, sequins and foiled glass beads. Still today the best way to show off a beautiful vintage full-length, or Cathedral-style veil is with the simplest of dresses.

Vintage veil styles

Shopping for a vintage veil can throw up all kinds of confusion in terminology and advice: some dealers stipulate that you should look at dresses only after deciding on the veil; others unequivocally state the opposite. When you can no longer think straight, bear in mind that these frothy creations are said to be as you should be on your big day: "light as dreams, strong as love."

Some types of veil

- Bonnet veil: worn over the face or thrown back from a hat or headpiece ☞

- Blusher veil: covers the face; bad form to wear during pregnancy

- Mantilla style: worn covering the face, as once common for Sunday church services

- Madonna veil: gathered at the back of the head to fall just beneath the shoulders

- Elbow length: touches the elbows for an extra misty impression

- Fingertip length: should extend to the ends of the fingers with arms outstretched

- Waltz style: also known as walking length, this veil stops mid-calf or at the ankle to allow for dancing

- Chapel length: skims the floor, and needs to be cut to suit the height of the bride

- Cathedral length: the showstopper, lightweight fabric extending to five yards or more behind the bride; necessitates a very simple gown

Popular vintage headdresses for securing veils

- Juliet or skull cap
- 1920s headband
- Floral circlet
- Tiara
- Crown
- Pill box
- Cloche cap

Making a Boutonnière

A classic single rose is a popular choice for making a boutonnière. Ideally, the bloom should be half open, not a tight bud, and shades of white, cream, or pale yellow will show up best against a dark formal jacket. Here the unusual green tinge of the petals has been complemented with a large variegated ivy leaf.

The personalized tags used here are made from textured paper finished off with a small eyelet, but you could buy small tie-on labels from a specialist stationer's. Arrange the boutonnières in a shallow box lined with tissue paper, to be distributed among the guests as they arrive for the ceremony; this task could be delegated to the bridesmaids or groomsmen. As a thoughtful touch, provide decorative pearl-headed pins to fasten the flowers in place.

MATERIALS

- *Cream roses*
- *Large ivy leaves*
- *Narrow ribbon*
- *Small tie-on/tag*
- *Gardening gloves*
- *Green florist's tape*
- *Rose wire*
- *Fine black pen*

TOOLS

- *Wire cutters*
- *Tape measure*
- *Scissors*

1 Trim the stem of the rose to approximately 3in/8cm long and, wearing gardening gloves to protect your fingers, remove any thorns.

2 Bind the stems of the rose and ivy leaf together with rose wire. Twist the two ends of the wire together and trim with wire cutters. Carefully flatten the ends of the wire against the stems.

3 Cover the stems with florist's tape, winding it upward from the bottom of the stems, then downward. Make sure the cut ends of the stems are covered completely so that they don't bleed.

4 Write the name or initials of one of the guests onto a tie-on. Cut a 12-in/30-cm length of narrow ribbon and thread on the tie-on. Make a knot in the ribbon a short distance from the tie-on.

5 Tie the ribbon in a bow around the boutonnière.

Flowers for Boutonnières

The well-dressed groom should sport a nosegay, or buttonhole, that echoes a key bloom in the bride's bouquet, much as the medieval knight who carried his beloved's colors into battle. Worn over the heart in this way, a flower connotes love. By the end of the Victorian era, groom's boutonnières had become almost as showy as the bride's bouquet: some foppish men would wear an entire bunch of lilies, which one might describe in the parlance of the time as being "quite too utterly utter." Here are some good choices for the modern man about town.

- Gerbera: select from a startling range of colors that even includes dayglo
- Sea holly: elegantly spiky
- Sprig of lilac: make sure it's in bud so it retains its form all day
- Rose: the classic choice; it should be just open
- Lily-of-the-valley: for old-fashioned charm and scent
- Double freesia: opulent without being showy
- Parrot tulip: just the right side of narcissism
- Ranunculus: blousy but still masculine
- Miniature sunflower: a rather modernist statement
- Dahlia: choose a pompom variety for urban cool
- Peony: a traditionally masculine flower in Japan that stands for wealth and good fortune
- Cardoon: keep it small; dried versions work well
- Rosemary and chile: a culinary note to highlight a good suit

All White

"Return, I implore thee, clad in thy milk-white tunic. Ah, What intense desire attends thy beauteous form. No Woman could not but tremble at its seduction."

Sappho

Although white has always been the color worn by brides in Japan, marrying in white elsewhere is a relatively recent tradition, only coming into currency toward the end of the eighteenth century. Until this time, brides simply wore a special "Sunday best" outfit—and the more fashionable the better, just like modern brides who take their inspiration from the catwalk and couture lines. A blue wedding gown was popular in the eighteenth century, considered the color of fidelity and enduring love, since it was associated with the Virgin Mary.

Wearing white became particularly fashionable following the wedding at the White House in 1828 of U.S. President John Quincy Adams' son John to Mary Hellen, who dressed in white satin, adorned with orange blossoms and pearls. In Britain, it was Queen Victoria, as ever, who established a lasting trend in 1840, when she became the first royal bride not to don the traditional heavy silver brocade gown shrouded by an ermine and velvet cloak. Daringly, she chose an all-white silk satin ballgown adorned not with precious stones, but with modest flowers, epitomizing the fresh, go-getting spirit of the age. Victoria's break with tradition was embraced by other young women keen to follow new trends at court, and by 1860 etiquette books on both sides of the Atlantic were declaring it de rigueur.

White has been thought a lucky color for brides ever since, representing purity, chastity, youthfulness, and the endless possibilities of the unmarked page. It hints at spirituality, and new beginnings, and has associations with the great goddess of pre-Christian worship in her form as maiden, who governed birth and growth and was linked with the new or waxing moon (an auspicious time for a wedding). Roman senators wore white togas as they went about their civic duties; the color was given the name "candor" and its attributes—integrity, innocence, sincerity, and freedom from malice or bias—still seem to transmit to the woman who puts on white satin or silk, chiffon or lace for her wedding day. And, of course, in the days before washing machines and hot water on tap, white signified affluence.

By the early years of the twentieth century, white had become further identified with innocence because it was the color of children's clothing, and of a wealthy eighteen-year-old debutante's "coming out" dress, worn with a chaste string of pearls further to highlight her innocence in the "season" of coming out balls and introductions at court that served as a marriage market. A bride's wedding day marked the last time she would wear such a pure color and such simple jewelry. From now on she was ripe for rich, womanly tones and "real" jewels.

Marry in white
you've chosen right
Marry in grey,
you'll go far away
Marry in black
you'll wish yourself back
Marry in red
you'll wish yourself dead
Marry in green
you're ashamed to be seen
Marry in blue
you'll always be true
Marry in pearl
you'll live in a whirl
Marry in yellow
you're ashamed of your fellow
Marry in peach
your love's out of reach
Marry in pink
your spirits will sink.

Twentieth-century rhyme

The Bridal Crown

Since classical times, a coronet of green leaves has served as a symbol not just of victory but maidenhood, worn by a young woman for the last time on her wedding day. The head is a potent site to crown with a circle, in many cultures a shape that encloses protective powers. Most often the bride's circlet was woven from orange blossom, traditional bridal flower of Europe and the Americas, or rosebuds—pink and red combined in southern Spain.

Rosemary is entwined into the circlet by the female relations of a Czech bride to ensure love, loyalty, and wisdom, and for remembrance of the family she is leaving—in ancient Greece scholars donned wreaths of the herb to stimulate the memory. Carnations, another choice for a bridal coronet, may have gained their name from the *corone* flower garlands worn around the head for Greek rituals.

In Norway the bride's gold or silver tiara is donated by her village and hung with tinkling spoon-shaped silver charms. Following the marriage ceremony in Finland, a similar gold crown enables love divination merriment: the blindfolded bride is ringed by dancing single girls. Whoever she ennobles with her crown will be next to marry. In the Orthodox Christian wedding ceremony, a crown reminds participants of the sacred nature of marriage: after exchanging rings, bride and groom are each endowed with a crown of gold or fresh flowers, tied together with ribbon. The crowns resemble the halos in the frescos adorning the church interior, underscoring the sacred state that marriage brings to ordinary men and women, and hinting at the eternal salvation to come in Heaven.

Orange Blossom

Orange blossom was the flower offered by the Roman god Jupiter to his wife Juno—queen of the Roman pantheon and beloved by brides—on their wedding day, and it is the flower still most associated with wedding wreaths in the West. The orange tree bears flowers and fruit at the same time, signifying chastity and fecundity in one, making it most appropriate for wedding celebrations. In its native China, the waxy, scented orange blossom stood for purity and innocence as well as being a symbol of fruitfulness, and in the language of flowers used by florists it still says "you are as pure as you are lovely."

Some accounts have it that orange blossom was first employed in European wedding rituals in France. Others say it arrived in Spain during Moorish rule, and here it still forms part of traditional hair decorations, especially in Andalucia, where it denotes happiness and fulfilment. But it was in Italy that its perfume was most honored, given the name neroli from its association with the famed beautifying rituals of Anne-Marie de la Tremoille, Countess of Nerola, a medieval village near Rome.

From the continent of Europe, the custom of using orange blossom at weddings spread to the Americas (early missionaries carried the plant with them to California) and Britain, where in the eighteenth century, sprigs were bound with silver lace and ribbon and distributed to the bride's friends in anticipation of the festivities to come. By the end of the nineteenth century, it had become so ubiquitous at weddings that the term "to gather orange blossom" became, for men, a euphemism for courting.

It was Queen Victoria—who else—who popularized the trend, including orange blossom in her bridal wreath in 1840. There followed a feverish embrace by brides of the blossom. It had pride of place on wedding circlets and bouquets, was pinned at the breast, throat, or waist, formed into corsages, and used in bunches to loop up sections of the wedding dress. At a time when many brides still wore their Sunday best rather than custom-made gowns for their wedding, sewing orange blossom onto the dress was a way to elevate its status for a day. The French couture houses Worth and Paquin always included a choice with their wedding gowns of silk orange blossom blooms for the wedding, and silk roses for wear on subsequent occasions.

Where real orange blossom was unavailable or out of season, buds and blooms were crafted from wax. So fine was the work that the pieces passed on to become treasured family heirlooms, even museum pieces, and their use only faded in the 1950s with the advent of mass-produced plastic. But the orange blossom remains with us, its image still beaded onto a thousand gowns, trains, and veils.

Vintage Style That Works

When choosing a vintage dress, don't be constrained by looking for wedding gowns. Try on 1930s bias-cut evening gowns, 1920s beaded shifts, 1950s prom frocks, and anything else that jumps off the rail. Then find a dressmaker to make alterations, perhaps updating styles with a satin sash, ornate silk corsage, beaded cape, or chiffon shrug. It's always best to team vintage with something modern to avoid looking like you've stepped off a film set: shocking pink killer heels will do nicely.

Bias-cut: Look for crêpe and silk-satin cut across the weave of the fabric in shades of Champagne, ivory, and eau de nil that clings to the body, emphasizing a beautiful butt and slim waist. Not for the timid or weight-conscious: as the fluid line of fabric moulds to the flesh, it accentuates lumps and bumps.

Simple shift dress: Straightforward flapper style chemises with a drop waist can take a lot of embellishment—fish-scale sequins and light-reflecting Swarovski crystals, Deco beading, and embroidery with tiny rocailles and bugle beads. Ornate decoration works especially well on shades of blush, oyster, and nude. Adorn with a corsage and beaded clutch bag.

Ruffles: For a bohemian feel, look for a skirt with ruffles around the hemline that kick when you step out and announce your arrival with swishes and rustles.

Silk chiffon: For the air of an ethereal waif in a slip of fairylike gossamer, look for sensual chiffon pieces in ruffled, ruched, and embroidered sheers. Cappuccino, pale pink, and olive green all team well with antique lace shawls and veils.

Empire line: With a high waist and figure-fitting silhouette, this style looks very feminine and flatters a petite figure. Its creator, Paul Poiret, in 1908 described his design's ability to emphasize a woman's moving form in its "undulating svelteness."

Greek column dress: Fortuny-style pleats and folds inspired by ancient Greek sculpture emphasize womanly curves and suit shimmering metallic fabrics. Search for sculptural drapery that hangs cleanly from the shoulders for that goddess effect.

New look: Dior's tiny waist, fitted bodice, and full skirt revolutionized postwar fashion in spring 1947 with a new femininity and frivolity after the utility fashions of the war years. These styles remain flattering for hourglass figures.

1950s swing style: Early 1950s "intermission" or "matinée" wedding dresses feature a tight bodice and impossibly full crinoline skirt that stops mid-calf, ideal for showing off a fabulous pair of shoes or for a dancing party, hence its alternative monikers, "cocktail" or "ballerina" gown.

Cocktail dress: Think 1950s curvaceous movie star, with a strapless bodice and fitted pencil skirt in jewel tones for temptress glamour.

White smoking jacket: Choose "le smoking" for Bianca Jagger cool (she wore one in 1971 for her wedding to Mick Jagger in Saint Tropez), teamed with a wide-brim hat.

Minimalist: Clean lines and asymmetric cuts suit grown-up women who know what they want and don't need to hide behind frills and flounces.

Wash that Man Right Out of Your Hair!

A ritual bath for the bride is an essential element of wedding celebrations across the Indian subcontinent and Middle East, and even lingers in Europe, where, on the morning of their wedding, French brides are urged to wash away any lasting thoughts of previous boyfriends as they take their last bath or shower as a single woman.

Traditional Jewish brides-to-be completely submerge themselves in a rainwater-fed pool of water, no part of the body touching the sides, not a strand of hair floating to the surface of the *mikveh*, or ritual bath. During her total immersion, the bride-to-be withdraws from the world, like the French bride, divesting herself of the trappings of her single life. The bride immerses herself seven times, forming a meditative ritual, during which the woman utters time-honored blessings that draw her closer to God and feed the spirit in preparation for her new role.

Before her wedding, a Turkish girl was traditionally accompanied to the steam baths by women from both sides of the family to be washed with rose-scented water, vigorously scrubbed with soap, oiled with perfumed unguents, and have hands and feet painted with henna. All the while, the women would feast on sugary pastries while engaging in gossip about the fairness of the bride's skin and her suitability for childbirth. In the Hindu tradition, both bride and groom are given a ritual bath on the morning of the marriage, after which they do not leave their respective residences until the time of the ceremony.

Prewedding Skin Scrub

Use this skin-exfoliating treatment—a traditional Indian beauty treat for brides-to-be—three days before a wedding. Its exquisite scent, based on essential oil of jasmine, lingers and is said to evoke both passion and compassion, and calm the nervous system. Perhaps this is why it is used in premarriage massage scrubs and body lotions from India to Java. The mango face mask is appropriate for brides-to-be since mango, India's king of fruits, is associated in folklore with lovers and desire. It's good enough to eat. Avoid during pregnancy and if allergic to dairy products.

Ubtan Scrub

1 tsp cumin seeds	½ tsp grated nutmeg
1 tsp sesame seeds	1 tsp mustard oil
6 saffron strands	2 tbsp sesame seed oil
2 tbsp gram (garbanzo bean) flour	6 drops essential oil of sandalwood
½ tsp ground turmeric	4 drops essential oil of jasmine

Maharani Face Mask

1 very ripe mango
1 tbsp natural yogurt

1 Make the ubtan scrub: grind the cumin and sesame seeds and saffron strands using a pestle and mortar or coffee grinder until a fine powder is formed. Combine with the gram flour, turmeric, and nutmeg. Drizzle in the mustard oil and sesame oil to make a paste. Stir in the essential oils.

2 Mix up the mask: peel the mango, slice the flesh from the stone, and purée in a food processor. Stir in the yogurt.

3 Pick up handfuls of the ubtan scrub and, using circular movements with your palms, rub it over every part of the body, from your heels up to the top of your shoulders.

4 Allow the ubtan to dry like a body mask for 10 minutes, sitting on an old towel. As you do so, apply the mango mask to your face, avoiding the delicate eye area.

5 Wipe away the face mask with a warm wet washcloth, then splash your face with cool water, and pat dry.

6 Rub your body with your fingertips, making small circular strokes to remove the paste. As it flakes off, feel how soft and silky it leaves your skin.

7 Step into a warm bath, strewn with rose petals, if desired, and luxuriate for 20 minutes before patting dry with a warm fluffy towel.

Lulur Body Scrub

For at least 500 years, courtesans in the royal palaces of Central Java have been bathed and pampered for forty days before their wedding with lulur, a skin-softening blend of sweet and spicy powders. This was thought to prepare mind and body for the wedding bed and even to aid conception.

To leave skin silky soft and glowing, use this treatment once a week (avoid during pregnancy and if allergic to milk).

2 tbsp baby rice	*6 drops essential oil of jasmine*
1 tsp ground turmeric	*2 drops essential oil of sandalwood*
2 tsp ground ginger	*handfuls of rose petals*
6–8 tbsp whole milk	

1 Make the scrub: combine the rice and ground spices, then moisten to a paste by adding the milk little by little, constantly stirring to prevent lumps. Drop in the essential oils.

2 Apply handfuls of scrub to your skin, massaging it in by making gentle circles up from heels to shoulders. Use an up-and-down scrubbing action over knees and elbows, heels and buttocks. Relax for 10 minutes sitting on an old towel while the paste dries on your skin.

3 Using small circular fingertip strokes, rub off the paste, exfoliating the skin as you do so. Splash handfuls of cool yogurt over your skin. Shower off.

4 Run a warm bath, scattering over handfuls of the rose petals. Luxuriate in the flower water for 20 minutes or so. To still damp skin apply a floral body lotion: look for one containing extracts of jasmine, rose, and geranium.

A Wedding Morning Ritual

This indulgent petal bath for your wedding morning employs skin-softening ingredients long associated with love and marriage—roses and rosewater, jasmine essence, and milk. As you lie in the bath, practice deepening the breath to relieve palpitations and a fluttering tummy.

Jasmine Milk Bath

12 tbsp milk powder
2 tbsp rosewater
6 drops essential oil of jasmine (omit during pregnancy)

2 drops essential oil of neroli
handfuls of rose petals, orange blossom, or jasmine

1 Place the milk powder in a large bowl and dilute with double the amount of cool water, adding the liquid gradually and stirring to prevent lumps. Stir in the rosewater and drop in the essential oils.

2 Run a deep, warm bath, pouring the solution into the water as you run the faucet. Just before stepping in, strew the petals over the surface of the water.

3 Lie in the bath for 20 minutes and start to watch your breath moving in and out. When you feel calm and focused, breathe in to the count of four, retain the breath for four, then exhale for eight. Take a recovery breath, if necessary, then repeat, working for 3–5 minutes in total. Try not to grasp at the breath; let the inhalation come naturally. Place a strainer over the drain when emptying the bath.

(HIM) I WEAR YOUR GOLDEN RING, MY DEAR,
SEE IT ON MY FINGER HERE,
I WEAR YOUR GOLDEN RING, MY DEAR,
SEE IT ON MY HAND.
AND IF THE RING WERE NOT FROM YOU,
NO OTHER RING I'D WEAR, MY DEAR,
AND IF THE RING WERE NOT FROM YOU,
NO OTHER RING I'D WEAR.

(HER) AND IF YOU HAD NOT MY RING,
ON YOUR FINGER, DARLING,
AND IF YOU HAD NOT MY RING,
STILL I'D NOT BE SAD.
SINCE LONG AGO ANOTHER RING I PUT IN YOUR HEART, DARLING,
SINCE LONG AGO ANOTHER RING I GAVE YOU, DARLING.

German folk song

Faith Rings

The first clasped hand *fede*, or faith rings, of which the Irish Claddagh is the best-known example, were Roman. They were embossed with two interlocked palms that stood for the customary handshake between elders of each family at the end of the wedding ceremony that ratified the contract: a hand-fast made a commitment binding. These rings, often smithed from the amuletic metal iron, were given by women to their intended as a token of trust that the agreed betrothal would take place. Other types of faith rings were used in Brittany, France, and Spain, where a clenched fist, or *higa*, was a symbol of fertility, and later English heart-motif rings featured a carved key (to the husband's heart). In eighteenth-century England, clasped-hand love rings were made in the form of interconnecting rings. Each could be moved separately, but never untied, fastening together when each hand was clipped over the central heart motif. These may have been reworkings of the legendary Middle Eastern wedding rings given to a sultan's wives eight hundred years earlier to keep them from mischief on his long absences. Each one was made of puzzle pieces that, once removed from the finger, were all-but impossible to reassemble. Other ring-shaped loyalty pledges included the popular nineteenth-century band that fastened with a buckle. If a young lady accepted the ring and fastened the buckle, it sent the message that her heart (and fate) was secured to her suitor's.

Left: *The Measure for the Wedding Ring*, by Michael Frederick Halliday

The Wedding Ring

The band of gold, a circle without beginning or end, is a powerful symbol of never-ending love, forged from the metal associated with the power and energy of the sun, gold.

Exchanging rings to mark a contract began with the Romans, who wore rings widely, men and women alike, as a sign of office, to ward off bad luck or cure ailments, with a seal to secure deals, or simply as a visual reminder of a pledge made. Circles occur over and over again in wedding lore across the globe—the tiny round cakes served on the wedding morning in the Orkney Islands, the circle dances of Eastern European weddings, the journey around the altar at a Greek Orthodox wedding, and the seven steps taken by a Hindu bride and groom around the holy fire. All represent the notion of eternity.

The ring finger

Until the beginning of the seventeenth century, wedding rings in England were worn on the middle finger of the right hand. Thereafter, the ring moved to the fourth finger of the left hand: Catholic custom has it that the thumb represents God the Father, the index finger the Son, the middle finger the Holy Spirit.

Other sources explain that the precious ring sits here for protection—the index and little fingers are half exposed and so vulnerable. More romantically, ancient Egyptian, Greek, and Roman physicians maintained that a nerve, or vein, of love, the *vena amoris*, runs from the fourth finger of the left hand directly to the heart. Ayurveda, India's ancient holistic healthcare tradition, teaches that it is the finger associated with the power of the sun. In Germany both bride and groom exchange rings, placed on the left-hand ring fingers, to mark their engagement. Known as *trauringen*, or trust rings, they are transferred to the right-hand ring fingers during the marriage ceremony. In India there is no tradition of wedding finger rings, but in the south, women might wear a heavy silver toe ring on the second toe of each foot as a sign of marriage.

Ring inscriptions

Inscriptions engraved into a ring are a secret known only to the giver, the wearer, and the engraver. Etched where they will touch the skin, they conduct their magical charge of good fortune to the wearer alone. The marks, which have been in use since Egyptian times (then they included good-luck motifs) can be as restrained as the couple's initials and the date of the wedding, or accommodate more intimate messages of devotion. During Europe's Renaissance there was a boom in silver "poesy" rings etched with secret sentiments that lasted up to the eighteenth ☞

century. Inscriptions on Roman rings dating from the second century BC also attest to the contractual nature of exchanging rings: the words record the nature of the marriage agreement signed in the presence of the emperor's image.

"With these rings I thee wed"

The Swedish bride is not truly married until she receives three wedding bands: one for the engagement, one for the wedding itself, and one for motherhood. Russian wedding rings, popular in the West, also comprise triple bands, often in different types of gold, perhaps yellow, pink (rose colored), and white, the three interlocked to form a single unit on the finger. Each D-shaped ring is a reminder of the holy Trinity of Father, Son, and Holy Spirit that are indivisible. Some rare Russian examples feature five rings.

After divorce, widowing, or separation they may be moved to the ring finger of the left hand. A gimmal ring, popular in Europe from the early sixteenth century onward, was similarly numerous, composed of two or three rings in different types of gold. But unlike the Russian example, the individual bands could be separated. Bride and groom would wear one each as a sign of engagement. If there were a third ring, a close acquaintance would guard it as a witness to the agreement to marry. At the ceremony, bride and groom's rings would be joined again on the bride's finger, with the optional third band worn by the groom.

"With these rings
I thee wed..."

Band of Gold

"The ring so worn as you behold,
So thin, so pale, is yet of gold;
The passion such it was to prove;
Worn with life's cares, love yet was love."

from "A Marriage Ring" by George Crabbe

Gold, the metal associated with the strength and purity of the sun, source of light and life, has long been considered most auspicious for wedding rings, since it does not tarnish.

In India it is thought to be a bringer of good fortune to all who wear it, and the higher the carat, the more fit for the gods it is. (Pure 24 carat gold is favored here; elsewhere 22, 18, or even 9 carat are preferred, the metal being harder and better able to stand up to wear and tear.)

When choosing a wedding ring, match the carat of the metal to your engagement ring, since a harder ring will rub against and erode a softer weight. Of course, modern brides shouldn't feel constrained by traditional ring choices. Wedding bands now come complete with diamonds and precious stones for extra sparkle, ornately edged with other metals, etched or smithed into intricate designs, made bespoke to reflect a couple's style, or reworked from much-loved family jewels.

Most important is for the band to feel so much part of you that you never remove it—a ring is said to prevent one's spirit from escaping the body and at the same time to prevent malevolent forces from disturbing the spirit.

Making a Table Centerpiece

A confection of frosted fruit, this tiered table centerpiece suits a winter wedding. Crystallized fruit in rich shades of red and pink is interspersed with leaves, bright orange kumquats, spiky lychees, and papery textured physalis, all standing on an antique pressed-glass cake stand that glints in the light.

MATERIALS

- *2 eggs*
- *Bag granulated sugar*
- *Glass cake stand*
- *Small pudding bowl*
- *Selection of fruit, such as nectarines, peaches, strawberries, lychees, kumquats, and physalis*
- *Sprays of green leaves*

TOOLS

- *Mixing bowl*
- *Egg whisk*
- *Coarse sieve*
- *Shallow dish*
- *Pastry brush*
- *Metal cooling rack*
- *Scissors*

1 Separate the eggs. Place the whites in the mixing bowl and beat gently with the whisk until frothy, but not stiff. Sift the sugar onto the shallow dish.

2 Using the pastry brush, coat the fruit with egg whites. Holding each piece carefully, gently roll in the sugar until completely covered, then place on the cooling rack. Repeat until you have frosted all the nectarines, peaches, and strawberries. Arrange in rows on the rack, making sure they do not touch. Sprinkle a little more sugar over patchy areas, then let dry.

3 Place the small pudding bowl upside down on the center of the cake stand to provide a support.

4 Shake each fruit gently to remove excess sugar. Arrange the nectarines and peaches in a circle around the pudding bowl. Make a second tier of large fruit, fitting them carefully in the spaces between the first layer to keep the arrangement stable.

5 Make a small circle of strawberries on top of the larger fruit, pointed ends outward. Finish the pyramid with a small cluster of lychees. Place more lychees around the edge of the cake stand in the spaces between the peaches and nectarines. Tuck kumquats into spaces above the lychees.

6 Peel the papery casing away from each physalis to reveal the round berry inside. Place them in spaces between the fruit in the second and third tiers.

7 Cut the foliage into single leaves and small sprays. Tuck these between the fruit at regular intervals.

"A marriage…makes of two fractional lives a whole; it gives to two purposeless lives a work, and doubles the strength of each to perform it."

MARK TWAIN

Scented Party Favors

Lavender Cookies

No commercial cookie can compete with a home-baked cookie, and the flecks of scented lavender make these extra special. Cut out in heart shapes, place two per guest in a cellophane bag, and tie with silk ribbon.

Makes 40

ingredients

½ cup/125g flour
½ cup/125g superfine sugar
1 tbsp ground almonds
1 egg yolk, gently whisked

1 tbsp lavender flowers,
  broken into individual florets
½ cup/1 stick/125g extremely
  soft butter

1 In a food processor, combine the flour, sugar, almonds, and lavender florets.

2 Mix in the butter and egg yolk until a firm paste, adding a little extra flour, if necessary.

3 Cover the dough in plastic wrap and place in the refrigerator to chill for 1 hour. Meanwhile, grease and flour two large baking sheets.

4 Divide the dough in quarters, and using a rolling pin, thinly roll out each in turn on a floured cutting board. Cut out with a heart-shaped cookie cutter and place on the baking sheets.

5 Bake at 190°C/ 375°F/Gas Mark 5, for 10 minutes, or until just brown at the edges. Remove before hard in the center. Leave on the tray to cool for a few minutes, then transfer to a wire rack.

Old-Fashioned Lemonade

Treat children at a wedding party to a flavorsome taste of the past that adults, too, will be clamoring to try.

Makes one pitcher

ingredients

1 large lemon
1 tbsp granulated sugar
tray of ice cubes
handful fresh mint leaves

1 Peel the lemon using a lemon peeler, being careful not to peel away the bitter white pith beneath the rind. Place the peel in a large glass pitcher.

2 Squeeze the lemon and pour the juice into the pitcher. Add sugar and pour over enough boiling water to dissolve the sugar, stirring well.

3 Add cold water and leave to cool. Add ice and the mint sprigs before serving.

"In all of the wedding cake, hope is the sweetest of plums."

19th-century dramatist Douglas Jerrold

Continental Wedding Cakes

The classic German celebration cake, *Baumkuchen* or tree cake, is so called because its thin layers resemble the rings of a tree when sliced. It recalls the tree of life found in so many religious traditions that unites heaven and earth, its roots deep in the soil, and branches stretching into the heavens. To the Norse people, *Yggdrasil*, a gigantic evergreen ash tree, towered over the world. It represented the universe, each of its roots reaching into a different world—the realm of the gods, the land of men and giants, and the place of the dead. This tree of knowledge gave Odin, the most powerful Norse god, the power of the runes, magical symbols that permitted mankind to record thoughts and make sense of the world. It also bestowed the gift of healing and the secret of war and peace.

In Scandinavia, the tree, or ring, theme is reflected in wedding cakes. Iceland's *kransakaka* comprises a pyramid of almond pastry rings stacked high and drizzled with white icing, the hollow center piled with chocolate and candy. In Denmark, the wedding cake is a towering stack of *kransekagemasse* marzipan rings formed into that most erotic of shapes, the cornucopia, essentially a sign of male and female sexuality coming together—its horn shape is filled to overflowing with voluptuous almond cakes, marzipan flowers, and sugar decorations. At the wedding banquet in the Asturias principality of Spain, bride and groom come together to offer each guest a piece of *cantelo*, ring-shaped wedding bread broken and served with a glass of wine.

The favorite celebration cake of France has been seized upon by modern wedding couples the world over in search of a breathtaking edible table centerpiece. Literally meaning "crack in the mouth," the impressive-looking croquembouche is formed from a towering stack of choux pastry puffs filled with cream and sugar, laced with brandy, and welded together with a caramel glaze that sets hard. If that weren't spectacular enough, it can be adorned with fresh flowers on the morning of the feast. Inexpensive to buy, and not difficult to bake (if you have a steady hand and stamina), this cake is recommended by wedding planners not just for its spectacular looks, but for the expense it saves on catering costs (serve it instead of pudding—each one should make around 200 servings).

Other contemporary cakes that double as dessert include glossy chocolate sachertortes finished with chocolate quills, Italian pastries filled with vanilla custard and fresh fruit, or sticky fudge cakes served with pitchers of pouring cream. Specialist cake designers and sugarpaste technicians now aim to fulfill every bride's romantic dream: edible masterpieces replicate fairy castles, animals, and monuments; flavors range from espresso to Mom's apple pie; and exquisite adornments steal the show— painstakingly crafted flowers, edible gold leaf, and colored frosting to complement dress, bouquet, or venue. None outshines Queen Victoria's cake. It stood 9 feet in diameter and was decorated with a sculpture of Britannia, two turtle doves, four cupids, and a dog.

Get me to the church on time!

Out with the Old

Around the world plates and glasses are smashed during wedding celebrations to mark the end of the old order and the start of a new life. In Germany, a raucous evening's entertainment the night before the marriage, featuring feasting, a wedding rehearsal, song, mime, and dance, culminates in the smashing of plates.

In Finland the bride takes to the floor for the first dance with a china plate on her head. Inevitably it falls and breaks; the pieces are taken to represent the number of children to come, as are the pieces of shattered glass of an Italian bride's smashed drinking vessel. To celebrate a Russian wedding, guests are expected to cast their toasting Champagne flutes or vodka shot glasses over their shoulders into a fireplace; smashing brings good fortune.

Such "excesses and disorders" had to be banned at toasts during wedding banquets in 17th-century Sweden because of shortages of glass and craftsmen and import restrictions. At the end of the Jewish wedding ceremony, after bride and groom have sipped from the second of two cups of wine, a ceremonial glass is wrapped in a napkin and crushed underfoot by the groom, while everyone cheers "Masseltov!"—good luck and congratulations. It echoes the Jewish lore that it's lucky to break a glass and portends the arrival of a baby. The German term *Polterabend* gives a clue to the reason for this smashing—loud noise is said to deter evil spirits attracted by the fecundity and lust for life of a young wedding couple.

Left: A Jewish wedding; a plate is about to be smashed for good luck.

Anna Karenina

by

LEO TOLSTOY

In the church there was all Moscow, all the friends and relations; and during the ceremony of plighting troth, in the brilliantly lighted church, there was an incessant flow of discreetly subdued talk in the circle of gaily dressed women and girls, and men in white ties, frockcoats, and uniforms. The talk was principally kept up by the men, while the women were absorbed in watching every detail of the ceremony, which always means so much to them.

In the little group nearest to the bride were her two sisters: Dolly, and the other one, the self-possessed beauty, Madame Lvova, who had just arrived from abroad.

"Why is it Marie's in lilac, as bad as black, at a wedding?" said Madame Korsunskaya.

"With her complexion, it's the one salvation," responded Madame Trubetskaya. "I wonder why they had the wedding in the evening? It's like shop-people…"

"So much prettier. I was married in the evening too…" answered Madame Korsunskaya, and she sighed, remembering how charming she had been that day, and how absurdly in love her husband was, and how different it all was now.

"They say if any one's best man more than ten times, he'll

never be married. I wanted to be for the tenth time, but the post was taken," said Count Siniavin to the pretty Princess Tcharskaya, who had designs on him.

Princess Tcharskaya only answered with a smile. She looked at Kitty, thinking how and when she would stand with Count Siniavin in Kitty's place, and how she would remind him then of his joke to-day.

Shtcherbatsky told the old maid of honor, Madame Nikolaeva, that he meant to put the crown on Kitty's chignon for luck.

"She ought not to have worn a chignon," answered Madame Nikolaeva, who had long ago made up her mind that if the elderly widower she was angling for married her, the wedding should be of the simplest. "I don't like such grandeur."

Sergey Ivanovitch was talking to Darya Alexandrovna, jestingly assuring her that the custom of going away after the wedding was becoming common because newly married people always felt a little ashamed of themselves.

"Your brother may feel proud of himself. She's a marvel of sweetness. I believe you're envious."

"Oh, I've got over that, Darya Alexandrovna," he answered, and a melancholy and serious expression suddenly came over his face.

Stepan Arkadyevitch was telling his sister-in-law his joke about divorce.

"The wreath wants setting straight," she answered, not hearing him.

"What a pity she's lost her looks so," Countess Nordston said to Madame Lvova. "Still he's not worth her little finger, is he?"

"Oh, I like him so—not because he's my future beau-frère," answered Madame Lvova. "And how well he's behaving! It's so difficult, too, to look well in such a position, not to be ridiculous. And he's not ridiculous, and not affected; one can see he's moved."

"You expected it, I suppose?"

"Almost. She always cared for him."

"Well, we shall see which of them will step on the rug first. I warned Kitty."

"It will make no difference," said Madame Lvova; "we're all obedient wives; it's in our family."

"Oh, I stepped on the rug before Vassily on purpose. And you, Dolly?"

Dolly stood beside them; she heard them, but she did not answer. She was deeply moved. The tears stood in her eyes, and she could not have spoken without crying. She was rejoicing over Kitty and Levin; going back in thought to her own wedding, she glanced at the radiant figure of Stepan Arkadyevitch, forgot all the present, and remembered only her own innocent love. She recalled not herself only, but all her women-friends and acquaintances. She thought of them on the one day of their triumph, when they had stood like Kitty under the wedding crown, with love and hope and dread in their hearts, renouncing the past, and stepping forward into the mysterious future. Among the brides that came back to her memory, she thought too of her darling Anna, of whose proposed divorce she had just been hearing. And she had stood just as innocent in orange flowers and bridal veil. And now? "It's terribly strange," she said to herself. It was not merely the sisters, the women-friends and female relations of the bride who were following every detail of the ceremony. Women who were quite strangers, mere spectators, were watching it excitedly, holding their breath, in fear of losing a single movement or expression of the bride and bridegroom, and angrily not answering, often not hearing, the remarks of the callous men, who kept making joking or irrelevant observations.

"Why has she been crying? Is she being married against her will?" "Against her will to a fine fellow like that? A prince, isn't he?" "Is that her sister in the white satin? Just listen how the deacon booms out, 'And fearing her husband.'"

"Are the choristers from Tchudovo?"

"No, from the Synod."

"I asked the footman. He says he's going to take her home to his country place at once. Awfully rich, they say. That's why she's being married to him."

"No, they're a well-matched pair."

"I say, Marya Vassibevna, you were making out those fly-away crinolines were not being worn. Just look at her in the puce dress—an ambassador's wife they say she is—how her skirt bounces out from side to sides."

"What a pretty dear the bride is—like a lamb decked with flowers! Well, say what you will, we women feel for our sister." Such were the comments in the crowd of gazing women who had succeeded in slipping in at the church doors.

Choosing Champagne

A glass of Bollinger or Cristal says occasion and style, with its honey-nut flavors and creamy complexity. Beware of Champagne's perverse labeling: brut is bone dry, extra sec/extra a little sweeter than dry; sec/dry medium sweet, and demi sec/rich the most sweet you're likely to find on the shelves. Whichever you choose, make sure to chill to 6–9°C/43–48°F.

Less costly options

If you can't afford for the Champagne to flow all day, save the good stuff for toasting, and supply less expensive sparkling wines, such as French méthode traditionelle, Spanish Cava, or Italian prosecco. Or be cheeky and ask each guest to bring a bottle to fuel the fires.

Non-alcoholic alternatives

Taste-test alcohol-free elderflower Champagne, sparkling grape juice, or old-fashioned homemade lemonade (see page 209). Alternatively, flavor sparkling mineral water with 1 drop essential oil of rose per large bottle.

Champagne cocktails

- Classic Mimosa: half-and-half, freshly squeezed orange juice, and Champagne.
- Kir Royale: a shot of cassis topped up with Champagne.
- Bellini: 3 parts (sieved) pulp of white peaches to 1 part Champagne, and a dash of brandy.

Traditional Wedding Toasts

The toast at the wedding reception is the first chance guests get to come together in wishing bride and groom every happiness for their future life. Raising a glass to the heavens for a blessing retains its powerful magic even in this secular age. Russia has the most intense toasting traditions (the wedding party is not considered a success until every guest is blind drunk), and these begin the night before, when the groom is urged to knock back a vodka toast to his bride in shot glasses arranged to spell her name. Pity the bride with a long name.

Popular toasts around the world

- "Masseltov!" Good luck and congratulations: shouted at Jewish weddings with the breaking of the bride and groom's toasting glass.
- "Skål!" Cheers: used at every occasion across Scandinavia.
- "Za molodykh!" For the newlyweds: the Russian toast that marks the beginning of the wedding feast.
- "Per cent'anni!" For 100 years: chanted at Italian wedding parties.
  "Evviva gli sposi!" Long live the couple: shouted especially by Italian men at every opportunity during the reception.
- "Que le Dieu bénit les mariés!" God bless the married couple.
  "Que le Dieu bénit les noces!" God bless the nuptials: old French toasts still used in Louisiana.
- "May you grow old on one pillow." Armenian wedding toast that has passed into common use.

Aphrodisiacs for Wedding Feasts

Foods of love with a long reputation for accelerating desire are just the thing to build into a wedding breakfast. These are seductive foods that don't fill to the point of sating, but do raise the spirits, enliven, and tempt.

Oysters: Considered the essence of feminine desire. Connote the abundance of the ocean and the ability to nurture precious pearls within a tightly shut shell.

Saffron: Beloved as an aphrodisiac everywhere, perhaps, like vanilla, because of its scarcity and extortionate cost. Saffron was cast into wedding beds, and used to dye bridal veils and scent aphrodisiac baths. In French Provence it flavors the *soupe de mariage* to ensure the groom's performance in bed.

Truffles: Beware: in 1368, the Duke of Clarence at his wedding to his Italian wife, ate so much of this delicacy (the truffle hills of Alba formed part of her dowry) that he died before reaching the wedding-night bed.

Dill: Believed to heighten desire, this herb was included in 19th-century wedding bouquets, then sprinkled over the feasting dishes, especially in Sweden.

Caviar: Comprising the fruit of the fish's loins, how could this not betoken fertility? Serve with a silver spoon on a crystal bowl over ice, with viscous cold vodka straight from the freezer or Cristal Champagne, the drink of choice of Russia's czars.

Sugar and Honey: In the Middle East, eating intensely sweet delicacies is associated with weddings, said to bring happiness and sweeten the match while providing protection from sadness.

"All the clothes worn by the bride might have been put in my pocket."

Eyewitness at Napoleon Bonaparte's wedding to the scantily clad Marie Louise of Austria in 1810

Jackie Kennedy's Wedding

When the twenty-four-year-old Jacqueline Bouvier walked down the aisle on her uncle's arm in Newport, Rhode Island, on a crisp sunny day in September 1953 to marry the thirty-six-year-old Senator of Massachusetts, John F. Kennedy, the young newspaper journalist was embarking on a very public life that started with the scrutiny of her wedding dress.

It made newsreel reports and the covers of magazines around the world. The dress was stitched from some fifty yards of ivory silk and featured a portrait neckline and bouffant skirt adorned with tiny wax flowers. It was dressed up with a single strand of pearls (a family piece) and a diamond leaf pin and bracelet, a gift from her bridegroom. On her head was her grandmother's veil of rosepoint lace, attached by a simple tiara of orange blossom and lace, and she carried a bouquet of scented gardenias and white and pink spray orchids.

The dress was the work of Anne Lowe, an African-American dressmaker from Alabama, who designed and created gowns for society ladies, including the du Pont, Roosevelt, and Vanderbilt families. She had been working in the profession since the age of sixteen, when her dressmaker mother died before finishing a wedding gown for the wife of Alabama's governor. Disaster struck when just ten days before the Kennedy wedding, Anne Lowe's New York studio and store was flooded, destroying ten of the dresses completed for the wedding, including the bridal gown. She replicated all in time for the marriage day.

Fall Floral Displays

- Bind bunches of wheat with red ribbon or plait to create corn dollies, traditional signs of fertility.

- Stand whole wheat sheaves on the floor. (Victorian brides had page or "straw" boys carry miniature versions down the aisle after them for fertility.)

- Fill vases with swatches of crab apples and rose hips.

- Build a pyramid of shiny apples in shades of russet and ruby.

- Stand single dayglo gerberas in bottles.

- Cut dahlias short to glow in zingy glass bowls.

- Bunch succulent sedum, ornamental in form even when not in flower.

- Seek inspiration from harvest festival displays: arrange decorative piles of pumpkins and gourds, marrows and corn cobs (another symbol of fertility, this time from Africa and Latin America).

- Adorn terracotta pots with stalks of artichoke heads.

- Plant bamboo in dark lacquered vessels. ☞

☞

- Make up rustic baskets of dried flowers: cornflowers and stacice, roses and hydrangeas.

- Purchase standard bay trees and transplant into smart urns.

- Display simple bunches of bright orange Chinese lanterns.

- Suspend bunches of drying flowers from the ceiling: roses, larkspur, and lavender, delphiniums and poppy seed heads, strawflowers, and hydrangeas. Match the flowers to the petals used for confetti.

- Scatter gilded pine cones (a sign of fertility and one of the emblems of the goddess Venus).

Fall Flowers for Bouquets

Dahlias: Pompom-headed or frilly, with a strong outline like a child's drawing of a flower. Fluorescent colors suit a modernist or 1950s-style wedding.

Chrysanthemums: No longer merely the cheap choice, florists now rate this flower for its lush heads and startling color range.

Michaelmas Daisies: A froth of violet blue, pink, or white delicate daisies on long stems that suit a country-style wedding.

Marigolds: Cheery gold color evoking autumnal sun; look surprisingly modern grouped together.

Hydrangeas: Mop-headed blooms in shades of pink and deep russet that look just as attractive dried.

Sedum: Stunning in unripe green or shades of mauve, madder, and even mahogany.

Sunflowers: Choose miniature heads for an unmissable bouquet that always looks contemporary; has associations with infatuated love.

Poppy heads: Add bold, modern interest to an arrangement even when the petals have fallen.

Sea Holly: The stems lend architectural form to a bouquet as well as glorious blue flowers and a silvery sheen.

Globe Artichokes: With their serrated leaves, these heavy heads look great with an innovative mix of flowers and decorative vegetables, such as chiles and baby squash.

Myrtle: Large black berries with an attractive scent and bluish bloom. Traditional in bridal bouquets since classical times.

When shall I marry?
This year, next year, sometime, never.
Who will he be?
Tinker, tailor, soldier, sailor, rich man, poor man,
beggerman, thief.
Where will we marry?
Church, chapel, cathedral, abbey.
How shall I get there?
Coach, carriage, wheelbarrow, dustcart.

What will I wear?
Silk, satin, cotton, rags.
How shall I get it?
Given, borrowed, bought, stolen.
And the ring?
Gold, silver, copper, brass.
Where will we live?
Mansion, cottage, pigsty, barn.

Love divination rhyme for cherry stones

Fruitful Unions

Marriages have brought together ingredients from across the globe to create taste sensations that become staple celebration foods in their new homes. When King Matthias of Hungary married Princess Beatrix of Aragon in 1486, she brought with her the recipe for a walnut-enriched sponge cake, thereafter known as *Piskóta*, that became the special-occasion cake still beloved by the Polish Diaspora.

Chocolate, too, which forms one of the most fashionable and crowd-pleasing wedding cakes *du jour*, also came to widespread use in Europe only as the result of a wedding. The ingredient became widely known following the marriage in 1615 of Louis XIII to the Spanish princess Anne of Austria. Tucked away in her dowry trunk, she brought with her to France a box of cocoa cakes. Aphrodisiac chocolate was linked with weddings since long before its discovery in the West. Aztec kings consumed chocolate in cups of pure gold before visiting their wives. It's still drunk in Central America to seal a betrothal, before and after the church ceremony.

New takes on wedding cakes

- Take three or more sponge cakes of increasingly smaller sizes and varying flavors, maybe lemon, vanilla, and passionfruit, cover in light butter icing, and decorate with crystalized rose petals and fresh flowers just before setting on display.
- Order a patisserie-created chocolate cake, asking for three layers in dark, milk, and white chocolate piled high with shavings and curls of extra fine chocolate.

Emma

by

JANE AUSTEN

…a few weeks brought some alleviation to Mr. Woodhouse. The compliments of his neighbors were over; he was no longer teased by being wished joy of so sorrowful an event; and the wedding cake, which had been a great distress to him, was all eat up. His own stomach could bear nothing rich, and he could never believe other people to be different from himself. What was unwholesome to him he regarded as unfit for any body; and he had, therefore, earnestly tried to dissuade them from having any wedding cake at all, and when that proved vain, as earnestly tried to prevent any body's eating it. He had been at the pains of consulting Mr. Perry, the apothecary, on the subject. Mr. Perry was an intelligent, gentlemanlike man, whose frequent visits were one of the comforts of Mr. Woodhouse's life; and upon being applied to, he could not but acknowledge (though it seemed rather against the bias of inclination) that wedding cake might certainly disagree with many—perhaps with most people, unless taken moderately. With such an opinion, in confirmation of his own, Mr. Woodhouse hoped to influence every visitor of the newly married pair; but still the cake was eaten; and there was no rest for his benevolent nerves till it was all gone.

Ice cakes,

spice cakes

all for tea,

We'll have

our wedding

at half

past three.

CHILDREN'S RHYME

Tiered Cakes

Wedding cakes must be tall, whichever tradition they come from—ornate royal-iced creations groaning layer upon layer on classical columns, Scandinavia's stacked edifices built from marzipan rings, the towering French croquembouche. The sheer height as well as the wealth of decoration suggests abundance, fruition, and opulence to the point of bad taste. Each of the numerous tiers is reputed to number one of the virtues that will keep the couple together: for example, steadfastness, fertility, togetherness, and friendship.

The tier idea seems to have originated in seventeenth-century France, where marriages were celebrated with two layers of cake: a richly fruited dark groom's cake wedded to a much lighter-textured bride's cake decorated with elaborate spun sugarwork, its whiteness reflecting the (hoped for) purity of the bride, and later echoing the color of her wedding dress.

In the U.S. in the nineteenth century, these two tiers were joined by an elaborately decorated third cake, perhaps baked with charms within, like the traditional Twelfth Night cake, in order to play love divination games. Finding a ring in your slice would foretell a marriage, a penny wealth to come, a thimble typecast the finder as an old maid or bachelor in waiting, and a button told of lost love.

Cutting into such a magnificently tiered cake is a high point in the wedding celebrations. Taking the knife together as man and wife as if with a single hand is a powerful symbol of unity and destruction of the old order. It was once said to be significant because it marked the first domestic duty a wife would perform.

The Wedding Cake

A byword for baroque extravagance, wedding cakes simply have to be rich in costly ingredients and lavish decoration. They are enriched with eggs, nuts, and seeds–elemental signs of new life in all cultures–and dripping with dried fruit and honey or sugar, emblems of extravagance that betoken a sweet and fruitful life to come.

All guests must eat of the cake, even those unable to attend the celebration, for only when every invitee, present and absent, has partaken of this symbol of new life, health, and prosperity can the marriage be thought truly sealed. The tradition of eating cake at the wedding feast is said to derive from a high-class Roman custom, in which parties to an agreement would share a cake baked from flour, water, and salt. Doing so made them eligible for high office.

But take out the cake's embellishments, the fruit and nuts, sugar and spices, butter and eggs, and you have the bread found in the loaf-breaking and sharing ceremonies that cluster around European weddings. This staff of life, made from wheat, ancient symbol of fertility, and leavened with yeast, that magic ingredient that ensures growth, is the forerunner of the wedding cake. The medieval English wedding ceremony ended with the breaking of a thin wafer of bread over the new wife's head to bring fertility; guests retrieved the crumbs as good-luck charms. Bread appears ritually in many traditions, offered with a sprinkling of salt to man and wife, who eat a crumb and sip a little wine to ensure their cupboards are never bare.

In Eastern Europe and Scandinavia, a specialty wedding bread has become a focus of the feast: the sweet Swiss *Brundlangskling* loaf; the Polish *syska* formed into propitious shapes such as animals, flowers, and pine cones like its neighbor, the Ukrainian *korovai*; the small ribbon-bedecked loaves that serve as party favors at a Russian wedding. (Parisian boulangerie Poilâne will bake bread rolls marked with your initials if you fancy adopting this tradition.)

The most elemental bread ceremony of all may well be the outdoor engagement ritual of the Poles. In a forest glade, well wishers ring the couple as they join hands over a loaf baked specially for the occasion. The couple's wrists are bound with a silk scarf, then words are said, the bread is broken and, dipped in a little salt, tasted by the couple. They each sip from a single cup of wine before the bride pours the remaining liquid onto the earth as a libation. And the strangest ingredient for a wedding cake? A bride's sweat.

In rural Russia, a bride would be accompanied to the *banya* or bathhouse to be bathed in milk, shaken with flour, then left in the searing heat of the steam room to sweat. The flour subsequently retrieved was a carrier for the most cherished of the ingredients in the wedding cake, sublime essence of bride.

Making a Napkin Ring

A simple sprig of dark ivy bound with sparkling glass beads and gauzy ribbon makes a memorable napkin tie. Or choose seasonal alternatives: decorative grasses, fragrant honeysuckle, jasmine, or autumnal red Virginia creeper—matching the theme to your floral arrangements.

MATERIALS
- *6-in/15-cm lengths of small-leaved ivy*
- *Rocaille beads*
- *Rose wire*
- *⅓-in/1-cm wide ribbon*
- *Linen napkins*

TOOLS
- *Wire cutters*
- *Flat-nosed pliers*
- *Ruler*

1 Cut a 10-in/25-cm length of rose wire. Thread on three beads and slide them down the wire to sit 1½ in/4cm from the end. Twist the beads with the flat-nosed pliers to keep them in place on the wire.

2 Thread more groups of beads at ⅔in/2cm intervals along the wire and twist in the same way. Leave 1½in/4 cm of wire at the other end.

3 Wrap a length of ribbon loosely around the ivy, leaving an 3in/8cm length at each end. Twist the beaded wire around the ivy stem and the ribbon.

4 Fold a napkin in half and roll it up.

5 Wrap the decorated ivy around the center of the napkin. Twist the ends of the wire together and flatten the ends with the pliers. Loosely knot the ends of the ribbon.

6 If necessary, store in a cool place, making sure not to crush the leaves.

Leaving the Ceremony

The processing of the bride and her party from her girlhood home to the place of the ceremony, veiled, shielded by flowers associated with good fortune, and under the guardianship of her nearest male relative, is a bittersweet moment.

In the past, it may have marked the last time a bride would see her family home before being "given away," and she was urged not to look back. The procession of bride and groom away from the ceremony, bride unveiled, accompanied now by bridesmaids, best man and ushers, both families, and joyful music has a markedly more festive air. In Germany the bridal couple process back down the aisle of the church each carrying a lit candle adorned with flowers and ribbons, beads and trinkets to celebrate their joyous state.

The procession away from the ceremony became ever more ornate as the nineteenth century drew to a close: in the late Victorian era, even the horses pulling the couple's carriage were drenched with floral tributes. Now, a couple might ask guests to join them in a procession by foot to the reception venue, the way decorated with bunting, floral garlands, flags, and streamers.

By taking part in a procession, each participant is showing, by putting their best foot forward, the strength of the new union, which brings together so many diverse families, friends, and colleagues. By traveling en masse in body as well as heart, every participant makes a public declaration of the commitment and strength of the new ties.

Russian Wedding Procession

It is perhaps in Russia that the post-wedding parade is most honored. Newly married couples and their witnesses take a two- or three-hour tour of the town's landmark sites in an elaborately decorated luxury car (it might even have a bride doll attached). They pose for a photograph at key beauty spots and leave flowers at each stop, but especially at war-grave memorials, to share some love and luck, and ask for the blessings of ancestors.

The pilgrimage to the town's key sites unites the couple with every other married couple in the town who have completed the same ritual procession, and all those who have gone before, in that blurring of time and place that accompanies celebrations that remain constant across the years. The outdoor procession around communal spaces also makes public the very personal vows just made. As the Episcopal minister petitions during the marriage ceremony, such a public declaration of love and responsibility should serve as a reminder to every married person present of their own vows, "Grant that all married persons who have witnessed these vows may find their lives strengthened and their loyalties confirmed."

That Kiss

"These two imparadised in one another's arms."
from *Paradise Lost* by John Milton

"You may kiss the bride," states the celebrant solemnly in more than enough movie weddings. Though these words are not included in the Christian or Jewish marriage services (where the first marital kiss might be coyly referred to as a "greeting" or "salute,") it's one of those sacred moments that sums up the day for many couples and their guests and, historically, does represent a legal contract of some sort. Since Roman times, a kiss has served as a means of sealing a bond.

It is perhaps in Russia that nuptial kissing gets most frenzied (and liquor-fueled) in the most ubiquitous of the wedding customs observed across the former Soviet Union. At the post-wedding feast there is a series of toasts to the new couple, usually with Champagne. At the first sip, one of the guests shouts out *Gor'ko!* meaning "bitter," in reference to the wine, and he is soon joined in a chorus of shouts of the same word. To remedy the situation—to sweeten the wine—the couple must kiss for as long as they can while the crowd counts out loud.

At the next toast and sip of wine, if it's considered that the first kiss wasn't long or passionate enough (and it never is), some wit shouts *Gor'ko!* and the couple are obliged to kiss again, for longer this time. And so it goes, after every toast, until the bride's makeup melts and the couple dissolve in laughter. In the U.S. guests often tap their glasses (and say nothing) in a humorous way. The bride and groom are expected to kiss when they hear the tinkling glassware.

Casting Confetti

All kinds of items shower the heads of newlyweds across the globe, from the obviously decorative (rice and rose petals) to the downright painful—ancient Romans cast nuts after the couple as they left the wedding ceremony; guests in the Czech republic prefer peas.

In India, throwing rice is one of the ten sacred "gestures" that sanctify husband and wife during the marriage ceremony, rice being a symbol of fertility and prosperity sacred to Lakshmi, goddess of wealth and success. To throw away something so precious is a sign of sacrifice that propitiates the gods.

Before rice was widely available in the West, wheat was the favored handful (for the same reasons) and it's still used in France. In Italy dried fruit, coins, and candy were the original source of the word *confetti*; in Romania, too, guests throw candy to represent the sweetness of married life, like the figs showered in Bulgaria.

Casting a carpet of rose petals before the bride as she makes her way down the aisle or into her new home is the traditional way in France and India to ensure her life will be sweet, and now petals are favored as the environmentally friendly way to shower the new couple in good wishes. Red and white petals thrown together are said to stand for the coming together of passion and purity.

"Green" Confetti

Pastel-toned paper luck tokens—horseshoes, petals, hearts, shoes, sweeps, birds, and rings—may look sweet, but they can stain a special dress irrevocably once wet and are banned by many churches and historic buildings licensed for weddings.

The most eyepleasing alternative is real petals, fresh or dried. You can buy supplies ready packaged from "real" confetti suppliers (search the ads in bridal magazines), who will gather petals to match a swatch of fabric from your gown. To save on costs, you might ask friends and neighbors to cut specified blooms from their garden or allotment. Hang them to dry, head down, in the months leading up to a wedding, then sort by color and store in boxes somewhere cool and dry, aerating them every few weeks by turning the petals by hand. As well as rose petals, look for delphiniums, which retain their color and shape when dried and come in hues to suit every bridal theme, from pure white to raspberry pink. Or try fresh or dried double peonies and camellias, cornflowers and marigolds, japonica and scabious.

Hand the confetti to guests wrapped in paper cones or silk sachets, or use as a decorative feature at the reception, filling wide glass bowls or woven baskets to the brim and emphasizing the scent by scattering over 3–4 drops of essential oil of rose or jasmine.

Make Some Noise

Causing a commotion outside the bride and groom's nuptial suite—or even inside it by meddling with the bed or standing around cracking jokes and pulling slapstick stunts—is one annoying custom that is common from Europe to China, where it's called the "spree" in the bridal chamber. Loud noise is thought to deter the bad spirits attracted to lucky wedding couples (a wedding dance floor might serve the same function today). In France rowdy guests at the wedding feast wait outside the newlyweds' room with pots, pans, and bells to bash accompaniments to bawdy songs, a custom known as *shivaree* or *charivari*. Tradition has it that the groom keeps a little something on hand with which to feed and water the crowd, and then they retreat. This is not to be confused with the English tradition of "rough music" or "scimity riding," ostracizing an adulterer or someone who has committed other sexual offences by gathering beneath his or her bedroom window at night to make such a disturbance with pots and pans that the presumed guilty are drummed out of town. The pots and pans, tongs and pokers, tin baths and cans that made up this "kiddly band" tended to be implements made of iron, an amuletic metal thought to prevent fairies and bad spirits from entering a home (hence the horseshoe on the door). Tin cans attached to the bumper of a getaway car share the same magic powers to keep the space spiritually sound.

JUST MARRIED

NOV 20

Les Misérables

by

VICTOR HUGO

The night of the 16th to the 17th of February, 1833, was a blessed night. Above its shadows heaven stood open. It was the wedding night of Marius and Cosette.

The day had been adorable.

It had not been the grand festival dreamed by the grandfather, a fairy spectacle, with a confusion of cherubim and Cupids over the heads of the bridal pair, a marriage worthy to form the subject of a painting to be placed over a door; but it had been sweet and smiling.

The manner of marriage in 1833 was not the same as it is today. France had not yet borrowed from England that supreme delicacy of carrying off one's wife, of fleeing, on coming out of church, of hiding oneself with shame from one's happiness, and of combining the ways of a bankrupt with the delights of the Song of Songs. People had not yet grasped to the full the chastity, exquisiteness, and decency of jolting their paradise in a posting-chaise, of breaking up their mystery with clic-clacs, of taking for a nuptial bed the bed of an inn, and of leaving behind them, in a commonplace chamber, at so much a night, the most sacred of the souvenirs of life mingled pell-mell with the tête-à-tête of the conductor of the diligence and the maid-servant of the inn.

In this second half of the nineteenth century in which we are now living, the mayor and his scarf, the priest and his chasuble, the law and God no longer suffice; they must be eked out by the Postilion de Lonjumeau; a blue waistcoat turned up with red, and with bell buttons, a plaque like a vantbrace, knee-breeches of green leather, oaths to the Norman horses with their tails knotted up, false galloons, varnished hat, long powdered locks, an enormous whip and tall boots. France does not yet carry elegance to the length of doing like the English nobility, and raining down on the post-chaise of the bridal pair a hail storm of slippers trodden down at heel and of worn-out shoes, in memory of Churchill, afterward Marlborough, or Malbrouck, who was assailed on his wedding day by the wrath of an aunt which brought him good luck. Old shoes and slippers do not, as yet, form a part of our nuptial celebrations; but patience, as good taste continues to spread, we shall come to that.

In 1833, a hundred years ago, marriage was not conducted at a full trot.

Strange to say, at that epoch, people still imagined that a wedding was a private and social festival, that a patriarchal banquet does not spoil a domestic solemnity, that gaiety, even in excess, provided it be honest, and decent, does happiness no harm, and that, in short, it is a good and a venerable thing that the fusion of these two destinies whence a family is destined to spring, should begin at home, and that the household should thenceforth have its nuptial chamber as its witness.

And people were so immodest as to marry in their own homes.

The marriage took place, therefore, in accordance with this now superannuated fashion, at M. Gillenormand's house.

We're a happy family.
With a great big hug
And a kiss from me to you
Now you know I love you true.

CHILDREN'S SONG

Love Letters

You don't have to write to record romantic sentiments on paper or ask formally for a hand in marriage.

Once paper had become widely available, from the seventeenth century onward, the art of paper-cutting allowed young men and women across Europe and North America to flirt and exchange tokens of love. Using scissors, knives, and even sheep sheers to cut and fold, emboss and tear, prick and punch paper, lovers would create elaborate works of art depicting hearts and flowers, love birds, and regional motifs.

The art is best known in Poland, where decorative *wycinanki* cut-outs of flora and fauna, garlands and rosettes were pinned to whitewashed walls and along beams, from cradles and cupboards, and as fringing on windows and shelves. Once the technique was taken to America by émigrés from Poland and the Ukraine, Byelorussia and Germany, it became a means of making love; the more intricate the design, the greater the affection shown. At some modern weddings a paper artist might circulate among guests cutting silhouettes as a memento.

Beaded letters

Zulu girls craft love letters to potential suitors in beads, stringing together tiny colored glass bugles to make palm-sized or smaller squares. Color and juxtaposition are used in much the same way Victorian women employed the language of flowers, each color and placement having a different meaning. White beads stand for pure love, red might symbolize passion or eyes sore from weeping, blood, or fire; blue stand for the sky, gossiping, or rejection. Meanings are so complex that only the intended can decipher them.

Tossing the Bouquet

A relatively recent American tradition (some date it to the 1950s), lobbing the bridal bouquet over your shoulder to be caught by an anxious scrum of women has been propelled through folklore and film into one of the prime duties of a bride to her unmarried friends.

In Victorian times, the bridal bouquet would be put on display in the entrance hall of the newly married couple's home for some days following the ceremony. Spanish brides still offer it to a statue of the Virgin. The custom of throwing the bouquet may have grown around the love fortune that attracts to a bride. For centuries it was lucky to procure a flower from the bouquet, either before the bride married by begging or stealing, or legitimately afterward: in some families, the bride would donate a sprig to each bridesmaid as they helped her change from wedding gown to going-away dress.

The act of breaking up the bouquet and casting it off seems to come from an older custom of throwing away items that symbolized one's non-married state, from stockings to shoes. This is not to be confused with casting worn slippers after newlyweds as they go away, or tying them to the getaway car, a way of wishing the couple good luck on their journey.

Throwing a shoe after someone setting out on a trip is a long-established way to court good fortune on their behalf, particularly practiced by fishermen's wives each time their menfolk set sail. Shoes also feature in love divination rituals: throwing an old boot at a willow tree on New Year's Eve is said, if the footwear sticks, to presage a wedding.

"Where's the man who could ease a heart like a satin gown?"

DOROTHY PARKER

The Language of Roses

Which color?

- Red: "I love you;" passionate love; flower of the Blessed Virgin
  Deep red: unconscious beauty
- White: "I am worthy of you;" sacred love; silent innocence; security and happiness; "flower of light;" a favorite of Native American brides
- Pink: perfect contentment; appreciation
  Dark pink: gratitude
  Pale pink: innocent love; grace; admiration
- Yellow: friendship; joy
- Orange: fascination; enthusiasm
- Coral: desire
- Peach: sociability
- Lavender: grace and refinement; love at first sight
- Purple: opulence and majesty
- Cream: thoughtfulness

In bloom or in bud?

- Single rose in full bloom: "I love you"
- Rosebuds: awakening love
  Red: pure and lovely
  White: girlhood; innocent heart
- Thorns removed: love at first sight
- With foliage: hope

Which variety?

- Hybrid tea rose: constant remembrance
- Cabbage rose: love's ambassador
- Damask rose: flawless
- China rose: grace and beauty ever fresh
- Dog rose: pleasure mixed with pain
- Rosa fetida: you are all that is lovely
- Rosa mundi: variety

Which form?

- Single rose: simplicity; perpetual love
  In full bloom: "I love you with all my heart"
- Two roses joined: commitment; a marriage to come
- Garland: virtue rewarded
- Bouquet in full bloom: gratitude
  12 roses: the ultimate declaration of love
  12 white roses: innocence; a secret
  50 roses: unconditional love
  Yellow bouquet: traditional for wedding showers
  Red and white bouquet or white roses with a red
  edging: unity
  Red and yellow bouquet: joyfulness
  Orange and yellow bouquet: enthusiastic passion
  One yellow and 11 red roses: love and passion

The Return of the Native

by

THOMAS HARDY

Across the stout oak table in the middle of the room was thrown a mass of striped linen, which Grandfer Cantle held down on one side, and Humphrey on the other, while Fairway rubbed its surface with a yellow lump, his face being damp and creased with the effort of the labor.

"Waxing a bed-tick, soul?" said the newcomer.

"Yes, Sam," said Grandfer Cantle, as a man too busy to waste words. "Shall I stretch this corner a shade tighter, Timothy?"

Fairway replied, and the waxing went on with unabated vigor. "'Tis going to be a good bed, by the look o't," continued Sam, after an interval of silence. "Who may it be for?"

"'Tis a present for the new folks that's going to set up housekeeping," said Christian, who stood helpless and overcome by the majesty of the proceedings.

"Ah, to be sure, and a valuable one, 'a b'lieve."

"Beds be dear to folks that don't keep geese, bain't

they, Mister Fairway?" said Christian, as to an omniscient being.

"Yes," said the furze-dealer, standing up, giving his forehead a thorough mopping, and handing the beeswax to Humphrey, who succeeded at the rubbing forthwith. "Not that this couple be in want of one, but 'twas well to show 'em a bit of friendliness at this great racketing vagary of their lives. I set up both my own daughters in one when they was married, and there have been feathers enough for another in the house the last twelve months. Now then, neighbors. I think we have laid on enough wax. Grandfer Cantle, you turn the tick the right way outward, and then I'll begin to shake in the feathers."

When the bed was in proper trim Fairway and Christian brought forward vast paper bags, stuffed to the full, but light as balloons, and began to turn the contents of each into the receptacle just prepared. As bag after bag was emptied, airy tufts of down and feathers floated about the room in increasing quantity till, through a mishap of Christian's, who shook the contents of one bag outside the tick, the atmosphere of the room became dense with gigantic flakes, which descended upon the workers like a windless snowstorm.

*Saturday night shall
be my whole care
To powder my locks and
curl my hair;
On Sunday morning my
love will come in,
And marry me then with
a pretty gold ring.*

English nursery rhyme

Meditation for the Night Before

Take a little time out of your heavy schedule for some stillness and reflection on this night of nights, and, above all, don't let the groom see you from now until you meet at the altar. Use this period of seclusion to remind yourself of who you are and what you bring to the marriage.

Sit quietly and turn within, thinking about your childhood, your youth, and all the events good and bad that brought you to this point and forged your personality. Then wipe the slate clean, focusing instead on the smooth movement in and out of your breath. Let only this occupy your mind, making it a sanctuary to retreat to, a place where there are no arrangements to make, promises to vow, or people to please.

Every time your mind wanders into anticipation of tomorrow, or concern for things left undone, bring your attention back to your breathing, and let it be still in this moment. In Java, on the night before her wedding, a bride sits silent and alone in contemplation for five hours. She waits to be filled by a divine spirit that comes in the form of an angel and remains with her for the five days of ceremonies that follow.

The same spirit enters all Javanese brides, making each one an archetypal figure, a symbol of the divine realm, and of God's presence in the commitment of marriage. In India, brides become an incarnation of the goddess Lakshmi, who bestows good luck, prosperity, and abundance on the new home.

The Wedding Night Bed

"May the nights be honey-sweet for us; may the mornings be honey-sweet for us; may the heavens be honey-sweet for us. May the plants be honey-sweet for us; may the sun be all honey for us; may the cows yield us honey-sweet milk."

From the Hindu wedding rites

Poet John Donne imagines the wedding bed as love's altar—for this is one of life's sacred nights—and as a cradle that nourishes new life, allowing it to grow and flourish. In China, the lovers' boudoir, or "mysterious room," is the place in which a bride discovers new mysteries about herself as she explores her ever-changing relationship with her husband.

Muslim brides being shown their new bedroom for the first time—a room that stays sacred to man and wife—may be asked to cut a red ribbon or garland before stepping across the threshold. Across the East on the nuptial night the bed is scattered with petals and adorned with garlands of flowers: jasmine in Bali and India, ylang-ylang around Indonesia.

Romans aspired to the example of the god Jupiter whose marriage bed is said to have been scattered with the costly petals of the immensely rare saffron crocus.

Scenting the Bridal Bed

What could be more romantic than crisp white bed linen perfumed with aphrodisiacal essential oils and scattered with handfuls of rose petals?

Jasmine-scented sheets for the wedding night

orange flower water
bed linen
essential oil of jasmine
handfuls of rose petals

massage oil blends featuring essential oils of neroli and ylang-ylang
sandalwood incense

1 Decant the orange flower water into a plant spray and spritz sheets and pillowcases before ironing.

2 Make up the bed with the ironed linen. Drop 6 drops essential oil of jasmine onto the bottom sheet, and 2 drops each essential oil on the edge of his and her top pillows.

3 Set the massage oils within reach of the bed. Smooth the top quilt or cover, then strew the rose petals over the top.

4 Before entering the room, light the sandalwood incense (used in India to cloud the bride and groom in a cleansing and blessing haze of aroma).

Choosing Linen

If white lace and flounces aren't your style for nights of passion, there are plenty more classic bedlinen options for a wish list to suit you and your man. No matter what you select, scent them with sachets of rose petals and lavender.

Traditional

- Lace-edged or embroidered antique Irish linen with drawn threadwork
- Crisp monogrammed Egyptian cotton
- Pure white poplin with self stripes or the most restrained of windowpane checks
- Open checks woven on a jacquard loom

Exotic
- Satin quilts in deep reds and chocolate browns
- Mirrored and embroidered Rajasthani throws, cushions covered in antique saris, and tasselled bolsters

Homespun
- Traditional French bridal patchwork quilt, worked all in white
- Spots teamed with checks and ginghams
- Washed-out Swedish Gustavian color schemes in gray-green, soft whites, and larch
- Pure wool Welsh blankets in plaids and checks, and Scottish tartans

Boudoir
- Paisley eiderdowns teamed with feminine floral designs in pastel shades
- Softest merino wool or cashmere throws

East Coast cool
- Checked cotton and thin stripes in shades of teal, duck egg, and off-white teamed with waffle-weaves
- Seaside stripes: combine wide and thin candy stripes and clashing primaries

French chateau style
- Toile de Jouy designs in pink, beige, and green
- Rococo scrollwork embroidery to match a wrought iron bedframe

Decorating the Table

Whether yours is a formal sit-down dinner or a more casual buffet where guests choose to sit or stand, get the table decor right and guests will immediately relax and get in the mood for a once-in-a-lifetime occasion.

Tablecloth

- Scatter fresh rose petals on white linen before guests are seated
- Customize cheap paper cloths with decoupage, calligraphy, or by sticking on scanned photographs
- Trail tendrils of ivy around place settings
- Place pots of colored pens on paper tablecloths and ask guests to pen a tribute, love poem, or limerick, or sketch their impressions of the day

Napkins and place settings

- Roll and secure with wide ribbon, ivy, or lengths of raffia, tucking in a single bloom or sprig of herb, and tying on a punched-hole name tag
- Screenprint bespoke napkins with a romantic quote or poem, names and date
- Place a flower beneath each overturned wine glass, with name attached to a tiny scroll of paper
- Scribe names onto richly colored fall leaves

Table centerpieces

- Press fresh flowers within decorative ice bowls and fill with summer berries
- Fill round goldfish bowls with fairy lights or jewel-colored candies
- Group fat church candles en masse for flattering evening lighting

Winter Floral Display

- Make festive evergreen swags using berried ivy, bay, rosemary, and fir adorned with scarlet ribbon

- Bundle together branches of winter berries

- Fill tall pitchers with berried holly

- Pile fresh figs and dates on pressed glass cake stands, leavening with a little greenery, such as bay leaves

- Suspend globes of mistletoe with an apple in the center

- Thread cranberries on twine to make garlands

- Bend wire into heart shapes and thread on shiny red chiles

- Make mountains of mandarin oranges, shiny leaves intact

- Wind wreaths of ivy (this signifies fidelity)

- Ring fat church candles with cinnamon sticks secured with a band of crimson ribbon

- Dry segments of orange (place slices in a barely warm oven for 5–6 hours) then thread into garlands

- Stud oranges with cloves to make pomanders, hanging them with crimson and green ribbon

- Fill cranberry and ruby glass vases with dark foliage and light with candles

- Assemble bowls of assorted nuts: cobnuts with husks attached, fresh almonds in season, the new season's walnuts

Winter Flowers for Bouquets

Anemones: Simple flowers in deep tones of red and purple or pure white with a tissue-paper-like velvet texture. Can be used with the delicate feathery foliage to impart an old-fashioned feel.

Lilies: Always elegant, suggesting purity and restrained elegance in tones of white and blush pink. Glossy Arum lilies have Golden Age of Hollywood glamour. The flowers are said to have sprung from the milk of the Roman goddess of marriage, Juno. Remove stamen to prevent pollen marking the dress.

Jasmine: Star-shaped flowerlets, bright yellow in winter and white in summer. Traditional in Hindu bridal garlands.

Gerbera: Available year-round in an astounding range of colors. Have a vibrancy that stands up well to modern themes.

Christmas Roses: Combine these waxy flowers in shades of off-white with silvery eucalyptus for a seasonal arrangement that doesn't resort to holly berries for interest.

Guelder Roses: When you want the eternal bridal favorite, a rose, and the summer varieties are not at their best, opt for these contemporary-looking sprays of berries.

Heather: Traditional for weddings with a Scottish flavor. The flower remedy helps ease an overwhelming concern with oneself and helps you connect with others.

Orchids: Fragile and mysterious, it is the essence of femininity despite the word's etymology—*orchis* in Greek means "testicle."

A Chaparral Christmas Gift

by

O. HENRY

The original cause of the trouble was about twenty years in growing. At the end of that time it was worth it.

Had you lived anywhere within fifty miles of Sundown Ranch you would have heard of it. It possessed a quantity of jet-black hair, a pair of extremely frank, deep-brown eyes and a laugh that rippled across the prairie like the sound of a hidden brook. The name of it was Rosita McMullen; and she was the daughter of old man McMullen of the Sundown Sheep Ranch.

There came riding on red roan steeds—or, to be more explicit, on a paint and a flea-bitten sorrel—two wooers. One was Madison Lane, and the other was the Frio Kid, but at that time they did not call him the Frio Kid, for he had not earned the honors of special nomenclature. His name was simply Johnny McRoy....

[Madison Lane] and Rosita were married one Christmas day. Armed, hilarious, vociferous, magnanimous, the cowmen and the sheepmen, laying aside their hereditary hatred, joined forces to celebrate the occasion....

But while the wedding feast was at its liveliest there descended upon it Johnny McRoy, bitten by jealousy, like one possessed.

"I'll give you a Christmas present," he yelled, shrilly, at the door, with his .45 in his hand. Even then he had some reputation as an offhand shot.

His first bullet cut a neat underbit in Madison Lane's right ear. The barrel of his gun moved an inch. The next shot would have been the bride's had not Carson, a sheepman, possessed a mind with triggers somewhat well oiled and in repair. The guns of the wedding party had been hung, in their belts, upon nails in the wall when they sat at table, as a concession to good taste. But Carson, with great promptness, hurled his plate of roast venison and frijoles at McRoy, spoiling his aim. The second bullet, then, only shattered the white petals of a Spanish dagger flower suspended two feet above Rosita's head.

The guests spurned their chairs and jumped for their weapons. It was considered an improper act to shoot the bride and groom at a wedding. In about six seconds there were twenty or so bullets due to be whizzing in the direction of Mr. McRoy.

"I'll shoot better next time," yelled Johnny, "and there'll be a next time." He backed rapidly out the door.

Carson, the sheepman, spurred on to attempt further exploits by the success of his plate throwing, was first to reach the door. McRoy's bullet from the darkness laid him low.

The cattlemen then swept out upon him, calling for vengeance, for, while the slaughter of a sheepman has not always lacked condonement, it was a decided misdemeanor in this instance. Carson was innocent; he was no accomplice at the matrimonial proceedings; nor had anyone heard him quote the line "Christmas comes but once a year" to the guests.

But the sortie failed in its vengeance. McRoy was on his horse and away, shouting back curses and threats as he galloped into the concealing chaparral.

The Captive Bride

Like the heroine of many fairytales, a bride is ripe for games of capture and intrigue. The Russian groom-to-be, like some storybook suitor set on saving a princess hidden in a tall tower, is compelled to climb all the steps of the apartment block to his bride, kept secure by female friends in her family's apartment. The elevator is blocked by acquaintances, and at each new stairway, the beau has to answer questions correctly about the bride's character, childhood, likes and dislikes, or pay a forfeit.

In Germany, the bride sneaks away to a bar (or three) with the best man, who holds her "captive" with glasses of wine or beer and treats allcomers to drinks until the bridegroom deduces the venue and bursts in to claim her with cash (and settle the bills). All around Europe, such playacting kidnappings are carried out with much jesting and games similar to those played at a bridal shower to test the memory and ingenuity of the man and woman, and their worthiness to marry.

In the Ukraine, bands of men will bar the entrance to the town hall where the wedding is held and demand a ransom payment before the nuptials can start. This seems to date from a time when the bride price was set by barter between families at the value of her ransom if kidnapped.

At modern Ghanaian weddings, similar bartering occupies hours of the wedding ceremony, as carriage clocks, weighty suitcases, airline tickets, and boxes of kente cloth are wheeled in and exchanged between family representatives—with much theatrical arguing until an agreement is struck. The seconds-long wedding then takes place.

Right: *The Major's Wedding Proposal*, by Pavel Fedotov

Who Not to Marry

Books on the correct mode of behavior for young women abounded in the late nineteenth century, many were preoccupied with the etiquette of catching a mate and marrying him (and the optimum ages at which to do so).

Urban myths did the rounds warning of the perils of a bad match, and so these manuals set out categories of cads waiting to ensnare impressionable young women. Despite the widely held view that one should marry for love, social standing mattered more. The warnings still ring true today!

How to avoid a bad husband:

- Never marry for wealth.

- Never marry a fop, or one who struts about dandy-like, in his silk gloves and ruffles, with a silvered cane, and rings on his fingers.

- Never marry a stranger, or one whose character is not known or tested.

- Never marry a man who treats his mother or sister unkindly or indifferently.

- Never, on any account, marry a gambler, (or) a profane person.

- Never marry a man who is addicted to the use of ardent spirits.

- Take especial and seasonable care that your children shall not have an ass for a father.

from *A True Friend*, American etiquette manual, 1870s

Making Thank You Cards

Acknowledge gifts with a personalized card that incorporates a scaled-down print of your favorite wedding photo, reduced on a photocopier or scanner.

MATERIALS
- *Thin marble-effect card*
- *Japanese tissue paper*
- *Copies of a 1½-in/4-cm square photograph*
- *Pearlized card*

TOOLS
- *Sharp pencil*
- *Metal ruler*
- *Craft knife*
- *Cutting mat*
- *Craft glue*
- *Glue stick*
- *Craft scissors*
- *Double-sided tape*

1 Cut one 4-in/10-cm square and another 3¼-in/8-cm square from the thin marble-effect card.

2 On the smaller square, mark a 1¼-in/3-cm square opening in the center with the pencil and ruler. Cut out on a cutting mat, using the craft knife and metal ruler.

3 Cut a 6-in/15-cm square of Japanese tissue paper. Attach the small square to the center of the tissue paper with a light coat of glue.

4 Make two diagonal cuts across the central square of tissue paper and cut off the outer corners. Fold the extra tissue to the back of the card and glue down.

5 Glue the photograph to the wrong side of the tissue-covered frame, then stick the frame to the center of the large square of marble-effect card.

6 Cut a 9½ x 4¾-in/ 24 x 12-cm rectangle from the pearlized card. Mark a point 4¾ in/12cm along each long edge and place it right-side up on the cutting mat. Score lightly between the two marks using the craft knife and metal ruler, then fold in half along the scored line. Stick the framed picture to the front of the card with double-sided tape, leaving an equal margin all around the card.

Threshold Traditions

"Love has a bunch of keys under its arm.
Come, open the doors."

13th-century Persian poet, Rumi

In India and China, and in the Christian world, brides do not just step into their new abodes, they are carried, lifted high, instructed which foot to use, and obsessively observed to ensure they get it right to prevent evil spirits harming bride and home.

The custom derived from the need for a girl entering a long-established family residence not to disrupt life with her own expectations, and to take on traditions. Before entering her new home for the first time, an Indian wife prays for a long-lasting, happy marriage, then kicks over a silver cup of rice with her right big toe (to step inside with the left foot first is thought to bring bad luck).

The spilling of a foodstuff, like the purposeful boiling over of milk when moving home, creates the impression of surfeit in the wish that the family will never lack sustenance. European brides were urged to plant magical herbs around the threshold. In England, sprigs of myrtle, orange blossom, and rosemary from the bride's coronet or bouquet, are said to flourish where women rule. Myrtle was best planted outside the front door; if it blossomed, it indicated a successful marriage. In Switzerland, it was a pine tree, symbol of immortality, fertility, and to the Romans, emblem of the love goddess Venus. In Holland, lily-of-the-valley at the front of the house recalls "many happy returns" of the wedding-day vows.

The Honeymoon

In the past, a honeymoon is said to have lasted one month—for the course of a single moon. Some sources claim it is named after the honey wine in which the couple were urged to indulge every day during this getting-to-know-each-other period (in ancient Teutonic times, a draught was thought to boost fertility).

The modern German term for honeymoon is *Flitterwochen*, or glittering weeks. Honey-laced confections accompany many nuptial traditions. Polish girls bake honey cakes to secret recipes to lure their sweethearts. In weddings across the Arab world, couples are not considered blessed until every guest has gorged himself or herself on decadent sweets. These include baklava and shredded pastries, halva and rice puddings, custards and sherbets, all intensely sweet if not honey-filled, and spiked with costly aphrodisiacs—cardamom and saffron, dates and rosewater, almonds, pistachios, and walnuts.

In Afghanistan, the word for betrothal, *shirnee khoree*, literally means "eating sweetness." Cynical commentators might suggest that the honeymoon period is named because following the excitement of the wedding, the early weeks of marriage come as an anticlimax, with love waxing, then waning, like the moon.